Introduction to Google's Go Programming

GoLang

by Prof. Dr. Orhan Gazi

Copyright

Orhan Gazi

Electrical and Electronics Engineering Department

Ankara Medipol University

Ankara, Turkey

ISBN: 9798863909929

© OG

Preface

In this book we explain Go programming language. Go was originally designed at Google in 2007. After its introduction, Go quickly gained popularity among programming languages. It is fast and lightweight programming language. Go is simple to learn and easy to read by other developers. It has a quicker compilation time. Go has automatic garbage collector that frees up memory when it is no longer needed. This feature eliminates the need for manual memory management, and it eliminates memory leak problem that can arise from manual memory management.

Go is a statically typed language, that is, errors can be caught at compile time rather than at runtime.

Go supports parallel programming and high-performance networking and multiprocessing applications can be achieved using Go programs. Concurrency can be achieved using go-routines and channels. Go-routines can be considered as light version of threads used in C programming. Using go-routines multiple operations can be performed at the same time. This makes Go an ideal programming language for developing high-performance and scalable network applications, as well as for performing complex computational scientific works.

Go was designed to write programs for networking, and cloud-based or server-side applications. Go has cross-platform support property, it can be compiled to run on many platforms, like windows, linux, mac and raspberry pi, etc. Go is used by many well-known companies, including Google, Uber, and Dropbox.

Go is an open-source programming language, and it is often referred to as Golang because of its former domain name, golang.org. Go has some advantages over C. C language uses stack memory to store the local variables, whereas, Go uses heap memory for local variables, and this eliminates some coding problems. For instance, when a function is terminated, local variables are destroyed in C programming, and if the function returns the address of a local variable, this creates a problem in C programming, whereas in Go programming this issue is eliminated by storing the local variables in heap memory. Syntax of Go is easier than many of the programming languages. Go has automatic data type detection feature for variables, and even pointers can be defined without specifying the pointed data type. For instance, a variable can be defined and initialized as

```
v := 30.7
```

and a pointer pointing to this variable can be defined as

```
ptr := &v
```

and variable data type and pointed data type is determined automatically by the compiler. It is clear that pointer declaration is quite easy in Go.

In this book we teach fundamental concepts of Go language. In chapter-1, data types are explained. Basic data types for integers are int, int8, int16, int32, int64 and their unsigned counterparts. Go has two data types for floating point numbers and these are float32 and float64. It is possible to define complex numbers in Go using the data types complex64 and complex128. There is only explicit type conversion available in go programming.

In chapter-2, we explain operators used in Go languages. Chapter-3 explains conditional statements. In chapter-4 functions, methods and interfaces are explained. Go functions are very powerful functions compared to the functions of other programming languages. They can return a multiple of values of different types, and due to the heap memory storage of the local variables in functions, addresses of local variables can also be returned by Go functions. Go methods are usually associated with structure data variables. Interface is a data types in Go, and this data type is a unique feature of Go language. Using interface data type and methods it is possible to write programs employing object oriented programming features.

In chapter-5 we cover structures. Accessing to the structure object elements using pointers in Go is easier in notation compared to other programming languages. Loops and arrays are covered in chapters-6 and 7. Slices are explained in chapter-8. Manipulation of arrays and slices are quite simple in Go language. Chapter-9 explains the maps in Go. Pointers are explained in details in chapter-10. Go-routines, mutex functions, channels, atomic operations which are used for concurrent program writing are covered in chapter-11. Finally, we explain file operations in chapter-12.

This book is an introductory book in Go programming. We tried to explain fundamental concepts of Go language using simple and neat examples. This book can be ready by anyone interested in computer programming and it can also be used as a text or reference book for one semester course in computer programming in colleges and universities. Finally as a last word, I dedicate this book to my younger brother **İlhan Gazi** who belongs to the category of good people.

Contents

Contents

Contents

Contents

Contents

Contents

Contents

Contents

Chapter-1

Data Types in Go Language

Abstract: In this chapter, we explain the data types used in Go programming. We use built-in functions Printf() and Println() to display the values to the screen. Go is a case sensitive programming language, and it has automatic garbage collector. Unused variables in go programming are not allowed even if they are used for illustrative purposes.

1.1 How to Write a Go Program

Every go program has a main function. For this reason, we first write the structure of the main function as in Code-1.1.

```
func main(){


}
```
Code 1.1

Inside the main() function, we can write go statements. We write a statement to display the "Hello World!" sentence to the screen as in Code-1.2.

```
func main(){

    fmt.Println("Hello World!")

}
```
Code 1.2

The Println() function used in Code-1.2 is defined in the package "fmt", we include this package using import keyword as in Code-1.3.

```
import "fmt"                              Code
                                          1.3
func main(){

   fmt.Println("Hello World!")

}
```

Finally, we import a special package called main which contains the code that can be built into an executable application, and we get the final form of the program as in Code-1.4.

```
package main                             Code
import "fmt"                             1.4

func main(){

   fmt.Println("Hello World!")

}
```

When the Code-1.4 is run, we get "Hello World!"

Example-1.1: Curly parenthesis must start right after the main().

```
package main                                                    Code
import "fmt"                                                     1.5

func main()
{ // error: curly parenthesis must be in the previous line

   fmt.Println("Hello World!")

}
```

Output(s): ./prog.go:5:1: syntax error: unexpected semicolon or newline before {

Example-1.2: The Println() function in the previous example can be used as in Code-1.6.

```
package main                                                    Code
import "fmt"                                                     1.6

func main(){

   fmt.Println("Hello ", "World!"); // semicolon is not needed

}
```

Output(s): Hello World!

Go is a case sensitive language, for this reason, the Println() function cannot be written as println().

Example-1.3: The Println() function can print the numbers as in Code-1.7.

```
package main                                    Code
import "fmt"                                     1.7

func main(){

   fmt.Println("The even numbers are:", 2, 4, 6)

}
```

Output(s): The even numbers are: 2 4 6

Example-1.4: The Println() function automatically inserts newt line '\n' character to the end of the printed sentence.

```
package main                    Code
import "fmt"                     1.8

func main() {

   fmt.Println("Hello ")
   fmt.Println("World!")

}
```

Output(s): Hello
               World!

Print() function can also be used to display a text on the screen. Print function does not automatically add the new line command as in the **Println()** function

Example-1.5: The **Print()** function does not insert next new line '\n' character to the end of the printed sentence.

```
package main                    Code
import "fmt"                     1.9

func main() {

   fmt.Print("Hello ")
   fmt.Print("World!")

}
```

Output(s): Hello World

Example-1.6: Semicolon can be used to write the lines of a go program on the same sentence. Code-1.9 can be written as in Code-1.10.

```
package main; import ("fmt")

func main() {

  fmt.Print("Hello "); fmt.Print("World!")

}
```
Code 1.10

1.2 Go Comments

Single line comments are written after //, whereas multiline comments are written between /* and */.

Example-1.7: In Code-1.11, we use single line and multiline comments.

```
package main
import "fmt"

func main(){
   // This is a single line comment.

   fmt.Println("Hello World!")

   /* This is
      multiline
      comment. */
}
```
Code 1.11

1.3 Go Variables

Variables are used to hold values. In Go programming, variables can be declared in two different ways. Variables can be declare

-   using **var** keyword

-   using := operator

With the **var** keyword a variable is declared as

$$\textbf{var} \text{ variableName } \textbf{dataType} = \text{initialValue}$$

and with := operator, a variable is declared as

$$\text{variableName } := \text{ initialValue}$$

14

where the data type of the variable is automatically detected by the compiler.

With the **var** keyword a variable can also be declared as

$$\textbf{var } \text{variableName} = \text{initialValue}$$

and in this declaration the data type of the variable is automatically detected by the compiler.

Note that there is **no space** between : and = inside the symbol := If space is placed between : and =, then error arises.

Example-1.8: In this example, we declare two variables and print their values.

```
package main                                          Code
import "fmt"                                           1.12

func main() {

  var a string = "Hello World!" // a is a variable

  var b int = 18 // b is a variable

  fmt.Println("a = ", a)

  fmt.Println("b = ", b)

}
```

Output(s):
a = Hello World!
b = 18

If a declared variable is never used inside a go program, compiler issues an error.

Example-1.9: The program gives an error, since declared variable is never used.

```
package main          Code
import "fmt"          1.13

func main() {

  var a int = 18

}
```

Output(s):

./prog.go:5:6: a declared and not used
Go build failed

1.4 Formatted Print Function: Printf

Printf () is the formatted version of the Print() function. The prototype of the Printf() function is as

```
func Printf(format string, a ...any) (n int, err error)
```

The function Printf() writes to standard output according to the format specifier, and it displays the error if there is, and returns the number of bytes written.

Example-1.10: The program in Code-1.12 can be written using Printf() function as in Code-1.14.

```
package main                                    Code
import "fmt"                                     1.14

func main() {

  var a string = "Hello World!" // a is a variable

  var b int = 18 // b is a variable

  fmt.Printf("a = %s \n", a)

  fmt.Printf("b = %d ", b)

}
```

The expression %s and %d in Printf function in Code-1.14 are the formats for string and decimal outputs.

Output(s):
a = Hello World!
b = 18

In Go, if you do not initialize a variable when you declare it, the variable is initialized by its default value.

Example-1.11: The variables in Code-1.15 are not initialized. Default initialization is done by the compiler.

```
package main                            Code
import "fmt"                             1.15

func main() {

  var a string

  var b int

  fmt.Printf("a = %s \n", a)

  fmt.Printf("b = %d ", b)

}
```

Output(s):
a =
b = 0

Example-1.12: In this example we declare variables using keyword **var** and operator :=

```
package main                        Code
import "fmt"                        1.16

func main() {

  var a int = 18

  b := 24

  fmt.Printf("a = %d \n", a)

  fmt.Printf("b = %d ", b)

}
```

Output(s):
a = 18
b = 24

Example-1.13: Data type may mot be written for variable definition with **var** keyword. Data type is never written for variable definition with := operator.

```
package main                        Code
import "fmt"                        1.17

func main() {

  var a int // data type is written here
  a = 18      // value assignment

  var b = 24 // data type is NOT written here

  c := 56 // data type is never written

  fmt.Printf("a = %d \n", a)

  fmt.Printf("b = %d \n", b)

  fmt.Printf("c = %d ", c)

}
```

Output(s):
a = 18
b = 24
c = 56

There are some differences between **var** variable declarations and **:=** variable declarations. These differences are

- **var** variable declarations can be done inside **main** function and outside main function,

- **:=** variable declarations can only be done inside main function,

- for **var** variable declarations, initial value assignment can be done after declaration,

- for **:=** variable declarations, initial value assignment must be done when declaration is made.

Example-1.14: In this example, we show that **var** declarations can be done outside **main** function.

```
package main                          Code
import "fmt"                          1.18

var a float32 = 2.45
var b int = 2
var c string = "Hello!"
```

```go
func main() {

  a = 4.5

  fmt.Printf("a = %.2f \n", a)

  fmt.Printf("b = %d \n", b)

  fmt.Printf("c = %s \n", c)

}
```

Output(s):
a = 4.50
b = 2
c = Hello!

Example-1.15: Variable declarations using **:=** cannot be done outside **main** function.

```go
package main                          Code
import "fmt"                          1.19

a := 2.45 // this is error

func main() {

  b := 8 // this is ok

  fmt.Printf("a = %.2f \n", a)

  fmt.Printf("b = %d \n", b)

}
```

Output(s): ./main.go:4:3: syntax error: non-declaration statement outside function body

1.5 Data Types in Go Programming

Go data types can be classified under three main categories which are

- Numeric data types :
  integer, floating point, and complex

- Boolean data types:
  true and false

- String data types

Let's explain these data types in details.

1.5.1 Numeric Data Types

Integer Data Types

The integer data types are listed as

```
int         Depending on the platform
            it can be 32-bit or 64-bit

int8        8-bit signed integer
int16       16-bit signed integer
int32       32-bit signed integer
int64       64-bit signed integer

uint        Depending on the platform
            it can be 32-bit or 64-bit

uint8       8-bit unsigned integer
byte        It is the same as uint8
uint16      16-bit unsigned integer
uint32      32-bit unsigned integer
uint64      64-bit unsigned integer

rune        It is the same as int32

uintptr     It is an unsigned integer type.
            It is used to hold a pointer value.
```

We can use the format %T to display the data type of a variable in Printf function.

Example-1.16: In this example, we define two integer data types and display their types using Printf() function.

```
package main                                Code
import "fmt"                                1.20

func main() {

  var a int8 = 12

  var b int64 = 89

  fmt.Printf("Data type for a is %T \n", a)

  fmt.Printf("Data type for b is %T \n", b)
}
```

Output(s):
Data type for a is int8
Data type for b is int64

If := is used to define a variable, its data type is determined depending on the assigned initial value.

Example-1.17: When := is used for variable declaration, data type is automatically determined by the compiler.

```
package main                                    Code
import "fmt"                                     1.21

func main() {

  a := 12;

  b := 24.89;

  fmt.Printf("Data type for a is %T \n", a)

  fmt.Printf("Data type for b is %T \n", b)
}
```

Output(s):
Data type for a is int
Data type for b is float64

1.5.2 Sizeof Function

In go programming Sizeof() function can be used to display the size of variables or data types in bytes. Sizeof() function is defined in the package "unsafe".

Example-1.18:

```
package main                                    Code
import "fmt"                                     1.22
import "unsafe"

func main() {

  var a int = 45

  var b uint16 = 78

  var c int64 = 674

  var p uintptr = 0xcABCDEEFF
```

```
    fmt.Printf("Size of int is %d \n", unsafe.Sizeof(a))

    fmt.Printf("Size of int16 is %d \n", unsafe.Sizeof(b))

    fmt.Printf("Size of int64 is %d \n", unsafe.Sizeof(c))

    fmt.Printf("Size of uintptr is %d \n", unsafe.Sizeof(p))
}
```

Output(s):
Size of int is 8
Size of int16 is 2
Size of int64 is 8
Size of uintptr is 8

Note:

Sizeof() function can be used with variables only, it cannot be used with data types, for instance Code-1.23 gives the error -- ./main.go:7:52: type int is not an expression—

```
package main                                                    Code
import ("fmt")                                                  1.23
import "unsafe"

func main() {

  fmt.Printf("Size of int is %d \n", unsafe.Sizeof(int)) // error

}
```

1.5.3 Float Data Types

Go programming language floating point data types are

float32 32-bit floating-point number, **range:** -3.4e+38 to 3.4e+38

float64 64-bit floating-point number, **range:** -1.7e+308 to +1.7e+308

These types comply with IEEE 754 standard.

Floating point values can be printed using the format %f, %g or %v where the latter two can be used to display the large numbers in scientific notation.

Example-1.19:

```
package main                                           Code
import ("fmt")                                          1.24

func main() {

  var a float64 = 7.3e+6

  fmt.Printf("Data type: %T \nData value: %f\n", a, a)
  fmt.Printf("Data value: %v", a)
}
```

Output(s):
Data type: float64
Data value: 7300000.000000
Data value: 7.3e+06

The largest real number that can be represented by float64 data type is approximately 1.79e+308.

1.5.4 Formats for Print and Scan Functions

The format %v is used to print the value of a variable, this is a general format. The format %#v is used to print the value of a variable prefixed by data class. For instance if we use %#v to print a hexadecimal number, number is displayed as
$$0 \times ...$$
for instance,
$$0 \times abc45$$

The format %v is interpreted for different data types according to

```
bool                                       %t
int, int8, int16, int32, int64             %d
uint, uint8, uint16, uint32, uint64        %d
float32, complex64, complex128             %g
string                                     %s
chan                                       %p
pointer                                    %p
```

Integer Formats

```
%b   base-2, binary
%c   the character
%d   base-10, decimal
%o   base-8, octal
%O   base-8, octal with 0o prefix
%q   a single-quoted character
%x   base-16, hexadecimal with lower-case letters
```

23

```
%X  base-16, hexadecimal with upper-case letters
%U  unicode format
```

Floating Point Formats

```
%e  scientific notation with small e, e.g. -1.56776e+89
%E  scientific notation, e.g. -1.56776E+89
%f  decimal point with no exponent, e.g. 6783.879
%F  the same as %f
%g  it is used for %e for large exponents
%G  it is used for %E for large exponents
%x  small-case hexadecimal e.g. -0x4.ab34ef+20
%X  upper-case hexadecimal notation, e.g. -0X4.AB34EF+20

%f      default width, default precision
%7f     width 9, default precision
%.3f    default width, precision 3
%7.5f   width 7, precision 3
%7.f    width 7, precision 0
```

1.5.6 String Formats

```
%s  for string or slice
%q  for double-quoted string
%x  small-case base-16
%X  upper-case base 16
```

Pointer Formats

```
%p                      hexadecimal notation, with leading 0x
%b, %d, %o, %x and %X   can be used with pointers
```

1.5.7 Complex Data Types

There are two complex data types in Go, and these are

```
complex64   complex128
```

Example-1.20: In this example, we define a complex number and print its value and type.

```
package main                          Code
import "fmt"                          1.25

func main() {

  var a complex64 = complex(-4.5, 8)

```

```
    fmt.Printf("a = %v\n", a)

    fmt.Println("a =", a)

    fmt.Printf("The type of a is %T", a)

}
```

Output(s):
a = (-4.5+8i)
a = (-4.5+8i)
The type of a is complex64

Example-1.21: In this example, we show alternative ways to define complex numbers.

```
package main                                    Code
import "fmt"                                     1.26

func main() {

  a := complex(-2.5, 5.3)

  b := 3 + 4i

  fmt.Printf("a = %g\n", a)
  fmt.Printf("b = %v\n", b)

  fmt.Printf("The type of a is %T\n", a)
  fmt.Printf("The type of b is %T", b)

}
```

Output(s):

a = (-2.5+5.3i)
b = (3+4i)
The type of a is complex128
The type of b is complex128

Example-1.22: Complex numbers can be added, multiplied and divided.

```
package main                                    Code
import ("fmt")                                   1.27

func main() {

  a := complex(-2.5, 5.3)
```

25

```go
    b := 3 + 4i

    add_res := a + b;

    mult_res := a * b;

    div_res := a / b;

    fmt.Printf("add_res is %v \n", add_res)

    fmt.Printf("mult_res is %.1v \n", mult_res)

    fmt.Printf("div_res is %.4v \n", div_res)
}
```

Output(s):
add_res is (0.5+9.3i)
mult_res is (-3e+01+6i)
div_res is (0.548+1.036i)

Example-1.23: The Code-1.27 can be written as Code-1.28.

```go
package main
import ("fmt")

func main() {

  var add_res complex128
  var mult_res complex128
  var div_res complex128

  a := complex(-2.5, 5.3) // complex128 by default
  b := 3 + 4i // complex128 by default

  add_res = a + b;
  mult_res = a * b;
  div_res = a / b;

  fmt.Printf("add_res is %v \n", add_res)
  fmt.Printf("mult_res is %.1v \n", mult_res)
  fmt.Printf("div_res is %.4v \n", div_res)
}
```

Code
1.28

Output(s):
add_res is (0.5+9.3i)
mult_res is (-3e+01+6i)
div_res is (0.548+1.036i)

1.5.8 Real and Imaginary Parts of a Complex Number

A complex number is written as
$z = a + bi$

where a is the real part and b is the imaginary part of the complex number.

Real and imaginary part of the complex number can be found using the go functions real() and imag().

Example-1.24: In this example, we illustrate how to display the real and imaginary parts of a complex number.

```
package main
import ("fmt")

func main() {

  a := complex(-2.5, 5.3)

  fmt.Printf("Complex number is : %v \n", a)

  re := real(a)
  im := imag(a)

  fmt.Printf("Real part of complex number : %v \n", re)
  fmt.Printf("Real part of complex number : %v \n", im)

  fmt.Printf("Real part of complex number : %v \n", real(a))
  fmt.Printf("Real part of complex number : %v \n", imag(a))
}
```
Code 1.29

Output(s):
Complex number is : (-2.5+5.3i)
Real part of complex number : -2.5
Real part of complex number : 5.3
Real part of complex number : -2.5
Real part of complex number : 5.3

Example-1.25: Size of the complex number can be calculated using Sizeof() function.

```
package main
import ("fmt")
import "unsafe"

func main() {

  a := complex(-2.5, 5.3)
```
Code 1.30

```
    fmt.Printf("Complex number is : %v \n", a)
    fmt.Printf("Size of complex number is %d \n", unsafe.Sizeof(a))

    re := real(a)

    fmt.Printf("Real part size of complex number : %v \n",
               unsafe.Sizeof(re))
}
```

Output(s):
Complex number is : (-2.5+5.3i)
Size of complex number is 16
Real part size of complex number : 8

Example-1.26: The size of a Boolean variable is 1 byte.

```
package main                                              Code
import ("fmt")                                            1.31
import "unsafe"

func main() {

    var a bool = true    // default is false

    fmt.Printf("a is : %v\n", a)
    fmt.Printf("Type of a is : %T\n", a)
    fmt.Printf("Size of Boolean variable is %v \n", unsafe.Sizeof(a))
}
```

Output(s):
a is : true
Type of a is : bool
Size of Boolean variable is 1

Note that Boolean refers to the name of a scientist who found Boolean data type. The word Boolean should start with capital letter.

Example-1.27: Logical comparison results are Boolean values.

```
package main                                    Code
import ("fmt")                                   1.32

func main() {
    a := 4;
```

```
  b := 5;
  c :=(a==b)

  fmt.Printf("c is : %v\n", c)
  fmt.Printf("Type of c is : %T\n", c)
}
```

Output(s):
c is : false
Type of c is : bool

1.5.9 Strings

Strings are the character arrays defined between two double quotation marks.

Example-1.28: In this example, we declare some strings and print their values and sizes.

```
package main                                    Code
import ("fmt")                                   1.33
import "unsafe"

func main() {

  a := "Hello";
  b := " World! ";
  c := a + b + "How are you?"

  fmt.Printf("a is : %v\n", a)
  fmt.Printf("c is : %v\n", c)
  fmt.Printf("Type of c is : %T\n", c)
  fmt.Printf("Size of a is %d \n", unsafe.Sizeof(a))
  fmt.Printf("Size of c is %d \n", unsafe.Sizeof(c))
}
```

Output(s):
a is : Hello
c is : Hello World! How are you?
Type of c is : string
Size of a is 16
Size of c is 16

1.6 Multiple Variable Declarations

It is possible to declare multiple variables in the same line. If data type is not written, variables belonging to different data types can be declared.

Example-1.29: In this example, we declare variables of the same type in the same line.

```
package main                              Code
import ("fmt")                            1.34

func main() {

  var a, b, c int64 = 5, 48, 0xAF6D

  fmt.Printf("a = %v\n", a)
  fmt.Printf("b = %v\n", b)

  fmt.Printf("c = %X\n", c)
  fmt.Printf("c = %#X\n", c)
}
```

Output(s):
a = 5
b = 48
c = AF6D
c = 0XAF6D

Example-1.30: Variables belonging to different data types can be declared in the same line if data type is not specified.

```
package main                              Code
import ("fmt")                            1.35

func main() {

  var a, b, c  = true, 4.56, "Hello!"

  fmt.Printf("a = %v\n", a)
  fmt.Printf("b = %v\n", b)
  fmt.Printf("c = %v\n", c)

  fmt.Printf("Type of a is %T\n", a)
  fmt.Printf("Type of b is %T\n", b)
  fmt.Printf("Type of c is %T\n", c)
}
```

Output(s):
a = true
b = 4.56
c = Hello!
Type of a is bool
Type of b is float64
Type of c is string

1.7 Scanf Function

The Scanf() function is used to get formatted input from the user. The prototype of the function is as

```
func Scanf(format string, a ...interface{}) (n int, err error)
```

where format string is used to specify input formats, and a ...interface{} are the parameters which receive given values.

Example-1.31: In this example, we get two numbers from the user and display them on the screen.

```
package main                                                    Code
import ("fmt")                                                   1.36

func main() {

   var a int
   var b float32

   fmt.Printf("Please enter one integer and one real number:")

   fmt.Scanf("%d", &a)
   fmt.Scanf("%f", &b)

   fmt.Printf("You entered %d and %f\n", a, b)
}
```

Output(s):
Please enter one integer and one real number:5 12.45
You entered 5 and 12.450000

1.8 Scan and Scanln Functions

The functions Scan() and Scanln() can be used to get input from the user.

Example-1.32: In this example, we illustrate the use of the Scan() function.

```
package main                                                    Code
import ("fmt")                                                   1.37

func main() {

   var a int
   var b string

   fmt.Printf("Please enter an integer and a string:")
```

```
    fmt.Scan(&a)
    fmt.Scan(&b)

    fmt.Printf("You entered %v and %v\n", a, b)
}
```

Output(s):
Please enter an integer and a string:45 "Hello!"
You entered 45 and "Hello!"

Example-1.33: When Scan() function is used to get the inputs, we can write each input on a new line.

```
package main                                              Code
import ("fmt")                                            1.38

func main() {

  var a int
  var b int

  fmt.Printf("Please enter two integers: ")

  fmt.Scan(&a, &b)

  fmt.Println("You entered", a, b)
}
```

Output(s):
Please enter two integers: 56
78
You entered 56 78

When Scanln() function is used to get inputs, we should write all the inputs in the first line.

Example-1.34: In this example, we illustrate the use of the Scanln() function.

```
package main                                              Code
import ("fmt")                                            1.39

func main() {

  var a, b int
```

```
    fmt.Printf("Please enter two integers:")

    fmt.Scanln(&a, &b)

    fmt.Printf("You entered %v and %v\n", a, b)
}
```

Output(s):
Please enter two integers:45
You entered 45 and 0

1.9 Constants in Go Programming

Constant variables have fixed data values which cannot be changed. A constant variable is declared as

```
const constVariableName dataType = value;
```

where dataType can be omitted, and in this case dataType is automatically determined by the compiler.

Example-1.35: Constant variable names are usually written in capital letters.

```
package main                                        Code
import ("fmt")                                       1.40

func main() {

  const A int = 19
  const PI = 3.14
  const BL = true

  fmt.Printf("A is : %v\n", A)
  fmt.Printf("PI is : %v\n", PI)
  fmt.Printf("BL is : %v\n", BL)

  fmt.Printf("Type of A is : %T\n", A)
  fmt.Printf("Type of PI is : %T\n", PI)
  fmt.Printf("Type of BL is : %T\n", BL)
}
```

Output(s):
A is : 19
PI is : 3.14
BL is : true
Type of A is : int
Type of PI is : float64
Type of BL is : bool

1.10 Go Keywords

In Go programing there are 25 keywords and these keywords cannot be used for variable names. The keywords are

```
break        case     chan        const    continue
default      defer    else        fallthrough
for          func     go          goto
if           import   interface   map
package      range    return      select
struct       switch   type        var
```

1.11 Type Conversion in Go

Go language does not support automatic or implicit type conversion as in C/C++. There is only explicit type conversion available in go programming.

Explicit conversion is performed as

$$dataType(val)$$

where the value val is converted to the type dataType. For instance, explicit conversion at initial assignment can be used as

$$var\ varName\ dataType = dataType(val)$$

Example-1.36: Explicit type conversion is illustrated in this example.

```
package main                                   Code
import "fmt"                                    1.41

func main() {

  var a int = 37
  var b float32 = float32 (a)

  fmt.Printf("Type of a: %T\n", a)
  fmt.Printf("a = %v \n", a)

  fmt.Printf("Type of b: %T\n", b)
  fmt.Printf("b = %.1f", b)
}
```

Output(s):
Type of a: int
a = 37
Type of b: float32
b = 37.0

Example-1.37: Explicit type conversion can be done in Printf() function.

```
package main                                          Code
import "fmt"                                          1.42

func main() {

  var a float32 = 6.78

  fmt.Printf("Float value: %v \n", a)
  fmt.Printf("Integer value: %v", int (a))
}
```

Output(s):
Float value: 6.78
Integer value: 6

Example-1.38: Explicit type conversion can be done for arithmetic operations.

```
package main                                          Code
import "fmt"                                          1.43

func main() {

    var a int = 45
    var b int = 4

    c := float32 (a) / float32 (b)

    fmt.Printf("c: %v \n", c)
    fmt.Printf("Type of c: %T", c)
}
```

Output(s):
c: 11.25
Type of c: float32

1.12 Global and Local Variables

Global variables are accessible at every part of the program, while local variables are accessible within its declaration scope. Global variables are usually declared before the main() function after the inclusion of packages.

Example-1.39: Global variables are accessible at every part of the program.

```
package main                                           Code
import "fmt"                                           1.44

var a int = 68  // global variable

func main() {

  fmt.Printf("Inside main part, a = %v \n",a)

  disp()
}

func disp() {

  fmt.Printf("Inside disp() function, a = %v \n",a)
}
```

Output(s):
Inside main part, a = 68
Inside disp() function, a = 68

Example-1.40: A local variable declared in main() function is not accessible inside other function.

```
package main                                           Code
import "fmt"                                           1.45

func main() {

  var a int = 68  // local variable

  fmt.Printf("Inside main part, a = %v \n",a)

  disp()
}

func disp() {

  fmt.Printf("Inside disp() function, a = %v \n",a)
}
```

When Code-1.45 is run, we get error.

Output(s):
command-line-arguments
./main.go:17:50: undefined: a

Example-1.41: A local scope can be defined using curly bracket pair. Local variables declared inside a scope cannot be accessed outside the scope.

```
package main                                          Code
import "fmt"                                          1.46

func main() {

  { // beginning of the scope

    var a int = 68 // local variable
    fmt.Printf("Inside scope, a = %v \n",a)

  } // end of the scope

}
```

When Code-1.46 is run, we get the output

Inside scope, a = 68

Let's add another Printf() function to the Code-1.46 as shown in yellow color in Code-1.47. When Code-1.47 is run, we get error, since the local variable a is not accessible outside its declaration scope.

```
package main                                          Code
import "fmt"                                          1.47

func main() {

  { // beginning of the scope

    var a int = 68 // local variable
    fmt.Printf("Inside scope, a = %v \n",a)

  } // beginning of the scope

  fmt.Printf("Outside scope, a = %v \n",a) // a is not accessible

}
```

Problems

1) What is the output of Code-1.48?

```
package main                                      Code
import "fmt"                                       1.48

func main(){

    fmt.Println("a =", 12, "\n", "b =", 56)
}
```

2) What is the output of Code-1.49?

```
package main                                      Code
import "fmt"                                       1.49

func main() {

    fmt.Print("a = 12 ")
    fmt.Print("b = 34")

}
```

3) Declare two integer variables with initial values 45 and 78. Print the values using Printf() function.

4) Fill the ... parts in Code-1.50

```
package main                                      Code
import "fmt"                                       1.50

func main() {

    var a string = "Hello" // a is a variable

    var b float32 = 18 // b is a variable

    fmt.Printf("a = ... \n", a)

    fmt.Printf("b = ... ", b)
}
```

5) Input two integers from the user calculate their summation and print the result to the screen.

6) Is it possible to declare variables using := operator outside the main() function?

7) What is the output of Code-1.51?

```
package main
import ("fmt")

func main() {

  var a float64 = 4.3e+4

  fmt.Printf("Data type: %T \nData value: %f\n", a, a)
  fmt.Printf("Data value: %v", a)
}
```

Code
1.51

8) Declare the complex number 4.5 + 6.7i in go, and print its real and imaginary parts.

9) What is the difference between Scan() and Scanln() functions?

10) Convert every integer to float32 in division expression 7/2, and obtain the result in floating point format and print it.

Chapter-2

Operators in Go Language

Abstract: In this chapter, we explain the operators used in Go programming. The Go operators can be classified as arithmetic operators, logical operators and bit-wise logical operators. Arithmetic operators are used to do mathematical calculations, logical operators can be used in decision blocks, bit-wise operators can be used for bit level operations.

2.1 Go Operators

Go operators are classified in four main categories which are

Assignment Operators
Arithmetic Operators
Logical Operators
Comparison Operators
Bitwise Operators

2.1.1 Assignment Operators

Assignment operator is the = operator. It is used to assign value to a variable. For example

```
var a int = 28
```

Augmented assignment operators are used for performing arithmetic operations and assignments at the same time. The augmented assignment operators are

```
+=   -=   *=   /=   %=   &=   |=   ^=   >>=   <<=
```

Example-2.1:

```
a += b equals a = a + b
a *= b equals a = a * b
a */ b equals a = a / b
```

Example-2.2: This example illustrates the use of the augmented division operator /=.

```
package main                                    Code
import ("fmt")                                   2.1

func main() {

  var a int = 24

  fmt.Println("a = ", a)

  a /= 4

  fmt.Println("After a /= 4, a =", a)
}
```

Output(s):
a = 24
After a /= 4, a = 6

2.1.2 Arithmetic Operators

Arithmetic operators can be listed as

```
+    Addition
-    Subtraction
*    Multiplication
/    Division
%    Remainder, i.e., Modulus
++   Increment
--   Decrement
```

The algebraic arithmetic operators, +, -, *, /, can be performed by the variables belonging to the same data types.

Example-2.3: In this example, the use of arithmetic operators is illustrated.

```
package main                                    Code
import "fmt"                                     2.2

func main() {

  a:= 12
  b:= 5

  r1 := a + b
  r2 := a - b
  r3 := a * b
  r4 := a / b
```

```
    fmt.Printf(" a + b = %v \n", r1)
    fmt.Printf(" a + b = %v \n", r2)
    fmt.Printf(" a + b = %v \n", r3)
    fmt.Printf(" a + b = %v \n", r4)
}
```

Output(s):
a + b = 17
a + b = 7
a + b = 60
a + b = 2

Example-2.4: In Go programming different data types cannot be used in algebraic arithmetic operators.

```
package main                          Code
import "fmt"                          2.3

func main() {

  a:= 12.6
  b:= 5

  r1 := a + b

  fmt.Printf(" a + b = %v \n", r1)
}
```

Output(s):
./main.go:9:11: invalid operation: a + b (mismatched types float64 and int)

Increment and decrements operations can be used alone. They cannot be used with assignment.

Example-2.5: In this example, we illustrate the use of the increment operator.

```
package main                          Code
import "fmt"                          2.4

func main() {

  a := 12.6

  fmt.Printf("a = %v \n", a)
```

```
a++

var b = a

fmt.Printf("b = %v \n", b)
}
```

Output(s):
a = 12.6
b = 13.6

Example-2.6: Increment and decrements operations cannot be used with assignment.

```
package main                           Code
import "fmt"                           2.5

func main() {

  a := 12.6

  var b = a++ // this is error

  fmt.Printf("b = %v \n", b)
}
```

Output(s):
./main.go:8:12: syntax error: unexpected ++ at end of statement

Note that there are **no prefix increment or decrement** operators as in C programming language.

That is, we don't have operations like

$$++a \qquad --b$$

2.1.3 Logical Operators

Logical operators are used between two logic expressions. The logical operators && , || and !
as explained in

```
&&  logical AND, a AND b is true if both a and b are true
||  logical OR, a OR b is true if one of a and b is true
!   logical NOT, NOT a is true if a is false
```

Example-2.7: This example illustrates the use of the logical OR operator.

```
package main                                    Code
import "fmt"                                     2.6

func main() {

  var a int = 5
  var b int = 13

  var c = (a < 6) || (b > 8)

  fmt.Printf("c = %v \n", c)
}
```

Output(s): c = true

Example-2.8: This example illustrates the use of the logical AND operator.

```
package main                                    Code
import "fmt"                                     2.7

func main() {

  var a int = 4
  var b float64 = 34

  var c = (a > 6) && (b > 8)

  fmt.Printf("c = %v \n", c)
}
```

Output(s): c = false

2.1.4 Bitwise Operators in Go Programming

The bitwise operators perform operations on each bit. The bitwise operators are

Operator	Name	Usage
&	AND	x & y
|	OR	x | y
^	XOR	x ^ y
<<	zero filled left shift	x << a
>>	sign filled right shift	x << a
&^	AND NOT	x &^ y

Example-2.9: This example illustrates the use of the bitwise AND operator.

```
package main                                              Code
import "fmt"                                              2.8
import "unsafe"

func main() {

  a := 0x0F // a = 00001111
  b := 0xFF // b = 11111111

  fmt.Printf("Types of a is : %T\n", a)
  fmt.Printf("Sizeof a is : %d\n", unsafe.Sizeof(a))

  fmt.Printf("a   = %08b\n", a)
  fmt.Printf("b   = %8b\n", b)

  fmt.Printf("a & b = %08b", a & b) // a & b = 00001111
}
```

Output(s):
Types of a is : int
Sizeof a is : 8
a = 00001111
b = 11111111
a & b = 00001111

Example-2.10: This example illustrates the use of left and right shift operators.

```
package main                                  Code
import "fmt"                                   2.9

func main() {

  var a int8 = -0x80 //  a = -1000 0000
  var b int8 = a << 3 // b = 0000 0000
  var c int8 = a >> 3 // c = -0001 0000

  fmt.Printf("a   = %08b\n", a)
  fmt.Printf("b   = %08b\n", b)

  fmt.Printf("c = %09b", c)
}
```

Output(s):
a = -10000000
b = 00000000
c = -00010000

Example-2.11: This example illustrates the use of and not operator &^.

```
package main                          Code
import "fmt"                          2.10

func main() {

    var a uint8 = 0xF0
    var b uint8 = 0x0F

    c := a &^ b

    fmt.Printf("a  = %#02x\n", a)

    fmt.Printf("b  = %#02x\n", b)

    fmt.Printf("c  = %#02x\n", c)
}
```

Output(s):
a = 0xf0
b = 0x0f
c = 0xf0

Note that in and not operator &^ there is NO space between & and ^.

Example-2.12: Let's consider the XOR operation in x ^ y, the result is 1 of x and y are different from each other, otherwise the result is 0. In Code-2.11, we illustrate the use of the XOR operator ^ in go programming.

```
package main                          Code
import "fmt"                          2.11

func main() {

    var a uint = 0x43     // 0x43 = 0100 0011

    var b uint = 0x26     // 0x26 = 0010 0110

    var c uint

    c = a ^ b //c = 0110 0101

    fmt.Printf("a = %08b \n", a )

    fmt.Printf("b = %08b \n", b )

    fmt.Printf("c = %08b \n", c )
}
```

Output(s):
a = 01000011
b = 00100110
c = 01100101

2.1.5 Comparison Operators

The results of the comparison operators are Boolean values false or true. The comparison operators are

```
Operator    Name                        Usage
==          Equal to                    x == y
!=          Not equal to                x != y
>           Greater than                x > y
<           Less than                   x < y
>=          Greater than or equal to    x >= y
<=          Less than or equal to       x <= y
```

Example-2.13: In this example, we illustrate the use of the comparison operators.

```
package main                                              Code
import "fmt"                                               2.12

func main() {

  a := 24
  b := 67
  c := 67

  r1 := (a != b)

  r2 := (b != c)

  r3 := r1 || r2 || (b < 0)

  fmt.Printf("Type of r1, r2, r3 are: %T, %T, %T\n", r1, r2, r3)

  fmt.Printf("r1 = %v , r2 = %v , r3 = %v", r1, r2, r3)
}
```

Output(s):
Type of r1, r2, r3 are: bool, bool, bool
r1 = true , r2 = false , r3 = true

Problems

1) What is the output of Code-2.13?

```go
package main                                    Code
import ("fmt")                                   2.13

func main() {

  var a int = 44

  fmt.Println("a = ", a)

  a /= 11

  fmt.Println("After a /= 11, a =", a)
}
```

2) If a is an integer, do we have ++a operation in Go?

3) What is the output of Code-2.14?

```go
package main                                    Code
import "fmt"                                      2.14

func main() {

  var a int = 0
  var b int = -5

  var c = (a == 0) && (b > 8)

  fmt.Printf("c = %v \n", c)
}
```

4) What is the output of Code-2.15?

```go
package main                                    Code
import "fmt"                                      2.15

func main() {

  var a int16 = 0x7FFF
  var b int16 = -5
  var c = (a | b)
  fmt.Printf("c = %v \n", c)
}
```

5) What is the output of Code-2.16?

```
package main                                    Code
import "fmt"                                     2.16

func main() {

    var a uint = 0x6F

    var b uint = 0xA8

    var c uint

    c = a ^ b

    fmt.Printf("a = %08b \n", a )

    fmt.Printf("b = %08b \n", b )

    fmt.Printf("c = %08b \n", c )
}
```

Chapter-3

Conditional Statements

Abstract: In this chapter, we explain conditional statements used in Go programming. Conditional statements, which are also called decision making statements or control statements, are used to select specific statements among a number of ones depending on some conditions. Conditional statements can be called as if statements. Conditional statements can be used in a nested manner. Besides, it is possible to construct ladder structures using conditional statements. Logical expressions are used in the conditional part of the if statements.

3.1 If Statement

The syntax of the conditional expression using only **if** keyword:

```
if condition {

    // Statements to be executed
    // if condition is true
}
```

The operation of the if statement is illustrated in Figure-3.1.

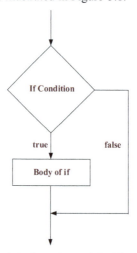

Figure-3.1 Flow chart of the if statement.

Example-3.1: This example illustrates the basic use of if statement.

```
package main                              Code
import "fmt"                              3.1

func main() {

  var a int = 10

  if (a > 0) {

    fmt.Println("a is greater than zero")

    fmt.Println("Inside if body")
  }

    fmt.Println("Outside if body")
}
```

Output(s):
a is greater than zero
Inside if body
Outside if body

3.2 If-else Statement

If-else statement is used to execute different statements depending on the value of conditional expression.

Syntax of **if-else** statement:

```
if condition {

    // executed if condition is true
} else {

    // executed if condition is false
}
```

The operation of the if-else statement is illustrated in Figure-3.2.

51

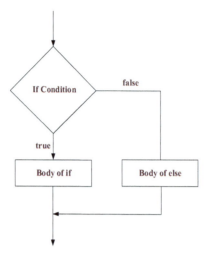

Figure-3.2 Flow chart of the if-else statement.

Example-3.2: In this example, the program displays a message according to the magnitude of the integer.

```
package main                                    Code
import "fmt"                                     3.2

func main() {

  var a int = 100

  if (a >= 250) {

    fmt.Println("a is greater than or equal to 250.")

  } else {

    fmt.Println("a is less than 250.")

  }
}
```

Output(s):
a is less than 250.

Example-3.3: In this example, the program gets an integer from the user and displays a message according to the sign of the integer.

```
package main                                                    Code
import "fmt"                                                      3.3

func main() {

  var a int

    fmt.Printf("Please enter an integer different than zero : ")

    fmt.Scan(&a)

  if (a > 0) {

    fmt.Println("You entered a positive number.")

  } else {

    fmt.Println("You entered a negative number.")

  }
}
```

Output(s):
Please enter an integer different than zero : -56
You entered a negative number.

Example-3.4: Conditional part is a Boolean expression.

```
package main                          Code
import "fmt"                           3.4

func main() {

  var a bool = true

  if a {

    fmt.Println("Inside if part ")

  } else {

    fmt.Println("Inside else part")
  }
}
```

Output(s):
Inside if part

Example-3.5: Conditional part can be a combines Boolean expression.

```go
package main                                    Code
import "fmt"                                     3.5

func main() {

  var a bool = false
  var b bool = true

  if a && b {

    fmt.Println("Inside if part ")

  } else {

    fmt.Println("Inside else part")
  }
}
```

Output(s):
Inside if part

Example-3.6: Comparisons produce Boolean results.

```go
package main                                    Code
import "fmt"                                     3.6

func main() {

  var a float32 = -5.6

  if a > 0 {

    fmt.Println("Inside if part ")

  } else {

    fmt.Println("Inside else part")
  }

}
```

Output(s):
Inside else part

Example-3.7: Modulus operator can be used in conditional expression.

```
package main                                    Code
import "fmt"                                     3.7

func main() {

  var a int = 10

  if a % 2 == 0 {

    fmt.Printf("%v is an even number", a)

  } else {

    fmt.Printf("%v is an odd number", a)
  }

}
```

Output(s):
10 is an even number

3.3 Conditional Ladder Structure (if else if ladder)

The syntax of the conditional ladder structure:

```
if condition1 {

// executed if condition1 is true

} else if condition2 {

// executed if condition2 is true

} else if condition3 {         .

    .

    .
} else {

    // executed if none of the conditions are true

}
```

Conditions are checked from top to bottom until, and when a true condition is met, the corresponding statements are executed.

Example-3.8: In this example, an integer is taken from the user and a message is prompted according to the sign of the integer.

```go
package main                                    Code
import "fmt"                                     3.8

func main() {

  var num int

  fmt.Printf("Please enter an integer: ");

   fmt.Scan(&num)

  if(num > 0) {

    fmt.Printf("You entered a positive integer.")

  } else if(num < 0) {

    fmt.Printf("You entered a negative integer.")

  } else {

    fmt.Printf("You entered zero.");
  }
}
```

Output(s):
Please enter an integer: 34
You entered a positive integer.

Example-3.9: In this example, letter assignments to the marks is performed using ladder conditional structure.

```go
package main                                    Code
import "fmt"                                     3.9

func main() {

  var  avg_mark int = 65;

  if (avg_mark <= 100 && avg_mark >= 90) {

    fmt.Printf("A+ Grade")

  } else if (avg_mark < 90 && avg_mark >= 80) {

    fmt.Printf("A Grade")
```

56

```go
    } else if (avg_mark < 80 && avg_mark >= 70) {

        fmt.Printf("B Grade");

    } else if (avg_mark < 70 && avg_mark >= 60) {

        fmt.Printf("C Grade")

    } else if (avg_mark < 60 && avg_mark >= 50) {

        fmt.Printf("D Grade")

    } else {

        fmt.Printf("F Failed")
    }

}
```

Output(s):
C Grade

Example-3.10: In this example, we use two Boolean expressions in the conditional parts of the if-else-if ladder structure.

```go
package main                                      Code
import "fmt"                                       3.10

func main() {

  var num int

  fmt.Printf("Please enter an integer between 0 and 100 : ")
  fmt.Scan(&num)

  if num >= 0 && num <= 25 {
    fmt.Printf("You entered a number between 0 and 25")

  } else if num >= 26 && num <= 50 {
    fmt.Printf("You entered a number between 26 and 50")

  } else if num >= 51 && num <= 75 {
    fmt.Printf("You entered a number between 51 and 75")

  } else {
    fmt.Printf("You entered a number greater than 75")
  }
}
```

Output(s):
Please enter an integer between 0 and 100 : 78
You entered a number greater than 75

3.4 Multi Conditional Structures

Multiple conditions are formed using the logical AND, and OR operators

$$\&\& \qquad \|$$

The OR operator gives true if one of the conditions is true whereas the AND operator gives true if all the conditions are true.

Example-3.11: In this example, multiple Boolean values are ANDed.

```go
package main                                    Code
import "fmt"                                     3.11

func main() {

  var a bool = true
  var b bool = false
  c := 12

  and_result := a && (!b) && (c>10);

  fmt.Println("and_result is :", and_result);
}
```

Output(s):
and result is : true

Example-3.12:

```go
package main                                    Code
import "fmt"                                     3.12

func main() {

  var a bool = true
  var b bool = false
  c := 12

  result1 := a && b || (c > 10);
  result2 := a || b && (c < 10);

  fmt.Printf("result1 = %v\n", result1);
  fmt.Printf("result2 = %v", result2);
}
```

Output(s):
result1 = true
result2 = true

Example-3.13: Another example for if-else-if ladder structure.

```go
package main
import "fmt"

func main() {

  var num1, num2 int

  fmt.Printf("Please enter two integers : ")

  fmt.Scan(&num1, &num2)

  if (num1 > 0 && num2 > 0 ) {

    fmt.Printf("You entered two positive integers.")

  } else if (num1 < 0 && num2 < 0 ) {

    fmt.Printf("You entered one positive and one negative integer.")

  } else if ((num1 > 0 && num2 < 0) || (num1 < 0 && num2 > 0)) {

    fmt.Printf("You entered one positive and one negative integer.")
  } else if(num1 == 0 && num2== 0) {

    fmt.Printf("You entered two zeros.")

  } else {

    fmt.Printf("One of the numbers is zero.")

  }
}
```

Code 3.13

Output(s):
Please enter two integers : 56 -67
You entered one positive and one negative integer.

3.5 Nested if-else Statement

The syntax of the nested if-else statement:

```
if condition1 {

    // executed if condition1 is true

    if condition2 {

      // executed if both condition1 condition2 are true

    }
}
```

Example-3.14: In this example, we illustrate the use of the nested if-else structure.

```
package main                                                    Code
import "fmt"                                                    3.14

func main() {

  var num int

  fmt.Printf("Please enter an integer between 0 and 100 : ");

  fmt.Scan( &num);

  if (num < 50)   {
    fmt.Printf("You entered a number smaller than 50. \n")

    if (num < 25) {
      fmt.Printf("You entered a number smaller than 25. \n")

    } else {
      fmt.Printf("You entered a number greater than 25. \n")

    }

  } else {

      fmt.Printf("You entered a number greater than 49. \n")

      if (num >75 ) {
            fmt.Printf("You entered a number greater than 75. \n")
      } else {
            fmt.Printf("You entered a number smaller than 75. \n")
      }
  }
}
```

3.6 Ternary Operator (?:) in Go

Most programming languages contain the ternary operator ?: which performs a task like an if-else statement. But, Go language does not have a ternary operator. The reason for this is the simple design choice. That is the code lines with ternary operator involving many terms are difficult to comprehend in a fast manner. In fact everything with ternary operator can also be done with classical if-else structure.

3.7 Switch Statement in Go

Switch statement is used to check the possible value of an expression, and when a match is found the corresponding statements are performed.

The syntax of the switch statement is as

```
switch expression {

  case exp1:
    //statements-1

  case exp2:
    //statements-2

  case exp3:
    //statements-3
        . . .
        . . .
  default:
    // statements-N
}
```

Example-3.15: The use of switch statement is illustrated in this example.

```
package main                                          Code
import "fmt"                                           3.15

func main() {

  var num int

   fmt.Print("Please enter an integer between 1 and 5 : ")

   fmt.Scan(&num)

  switch num {

    case 1:
       fmt.Println("You entered 1")
```

```go
    case 2:
      fmt.Println("You entered 2")

    case 3:
      fmt.Println("You entered 3")

    case 4:
      fmt.Println("You entered 4")

    case 5:
      fmt.Println("You entered 5")

    default:
      fmt.Println("You did not enter a number between 1 and 5")
  }
}
```

Output(s):
Please enter an integer between 1 and 5 : 8
You did not enter a number between 1 and 5

Example-3.16: More than one line can be written after **case** keyword.

```go
package main                                                Code
import "fmt"                                                3.16

func main() {

  var num int

    fmt.Print("Please enter an integer from 1 to 9 (inclusive) : ")

    fmt.Scan(&num)

  switch num {

    case 0, 2, 4, 6, 8:
      fmt.Print("You entered even number ")
      fmt.Print(num)

    case 1, 3, 5, 7, 9:
      fmt.Print("You entered odd number ")
      fmt.Print(num)

    default:
      fmt.Println("You did not enter an integer in [1-9] ")
  }
}
```

Output(s):
Please enter an integer from 1 to 9 (inclusive) : 5
You entered odd number 5

3.7.1 The fallthrough Keyword

The fallthrough keyword passes the execution to the next case. Other cases after the matching case can be executed, if we use fallthrough keyword inside the case statement.

Example-3.17: In this example, we use one fallthrough keyword, and we get two outputs.

```go
package main                              Code
import "fmt"                              3.17

func main() {

  var num int = 2

  switch num {

    case 1:
      fmt.Println("Number is 1")

    case 2:
      fmt.Println("Number is 2")
      fallthrough

    case 3:
      fmt.Println("Number is 3")

    case 4:
      fmt.Println("Number is 4")

    case 5:
      fmt.Println("Number is 5
  }
}
```

Output(s):
Number is 2
Number is 3

Example-3.18: In this example, we use two fallthrough keywords, and we get three outputs.

```go
package main                                    Code
import "fmt"                                     3.18

func main() {

  var num int = 2

  switch num {

    case 1:
       fmt.Println("Number is 1")

    case 2:
       fmt.Println("Number is 2")
       fallthrough

    case 3:
       fmt.Println("Number is 3")
       fallthrough

    case 4:
       fmt.Println("Number is 4")

    case 5:
       fmt.Println("Number is 5")
  }
}
```

Output(s):
Number is 2
Number is 3
Number is 4

3.7.2 The Switch Statement with Variable Initializer

The switch statement can contain an initializer part. The syntax is as

```go
switch initializer; expression {

  case exp1:
    //statements-1

  case exp2:
    //statements-2
        ...
  default:
    // statements-N
}
```

64

Example-3.19: In this example, we use the switch statement with initializer part.

```
package main                          Code
import "fmt"                          3.19

func main() {

  var num int

  switch num = 2; num {

    case 1:
      fmt.Println("Number is 1")

    case 2:
      fmt.Println("Number is 2")

    case 3:
      fmt.Println("Number is 3")

    case 4:
      fmt.Println("Number is 4")
  }
}
```

Output(s):
Number is 2

3.7.3 The Switch Statement without Switch Expression

Switch statement can be used without switch expression and, Boolean expressions can be used for case expressions.

Example-3.20: In this example, we use switch statement without switch expressions and we use Boolean expressions for inside case parts.

```
package main                          Code
import "fmt"                          3.20

func main() {

  var num int = 8

  switch {
    case num < 0:
      fmt.Println("Number is less than zero")

    case num > 0:
      fmt.Println("Number is greater than zero")
```

```
      case num == 0:
        fmt.Println("Number is zero")

      default:
        fmt.Println("Default comment")
      }
}
```

Output(s):
Number is greater than zero

3.7.4 Type Switches in Go

Type switch is used to compare types rather than values. When the data type is matched, the corresponding case statements are executed.

Example-3.21: In this example, type switch statement is illustrated.

```
package main                                              Code
import "fmt"                                              3.21

func main() {

  var num interface{} = 2.4

  switch data := num.(type) {

    case int64:
      fmt.Println("Data type is integer, number is:", data)

    case float64:
      fmt.Println("Data type is float, number is:", data)

    default:
      fmt.Println("Type is unknown!")
    }
}
```

Output(s):
Data type is float, number is: 2.4

Example-3.22: In this example, we illustrate how to use an integer variable with type switch expression.

```
package main                                          Code
import "fmt"                                          3.22

func main() {

  var a int64 = 65

  var num interface{} = a

  switch data := num.(type) {

    case int64:
      fmt.Println("Data type is integer, number is :", data)

    case float64:
      fmt.Println("Data type is float:, number is :", data)

    case string:
      fmt.Println("Type is a string:, string is :", data)

    case nil:
      fmt.Println("Type is nil.")

    case bool:
      fmt.Println("Type is a bool:", data)

    default:
      fmt.Println("Type is unknown!")
    }
}
```

Output(s):
Data type is integer, number is : 65

Problems

1) What is the output of Code-3.23?

```
package main                                    Code
import "fmt"                                     3.23

func main() {

  var a bool = false
  var b bool = true
  var c bool = true

  if a || b && c {

    fmt.Println("Inside if part ")

  } else {

    fmt.Println("Inside else part")

  }
}
```

2) Write a program which gets an integer from user and gives information whether the integer is divisible by 3 or not.

3) What is the output of Code-3.24?

```
package main                                    Code
import "fmt"                                     3.24

func main() {

  var a bool = false
  var b bool = false
  c := 0

  and_result := a || (!b) && (c>10);

  fmt.Println("and_result is :", and_result);
}
```

4) Is there ternary operator (?:) in Go ?

5) What is the output of Code-3.25?

```
package main                              Code
import "fmt"                              3.25

func main() {

  var num int = 3

  switch num {

    case 1:
      fmt.Println("Number is 1")

    case 2:
      fmt.Println("Number is 2")
      fallthrough

    case 3:
      fmt.Println("Number is 3")
      fallthrough

    case 4:
      fmt.Println("Number is 4")
      fallthrough

    case 5:
      fmt.Println("Number is 5")
  }
}
```

6) What is the output of Code-3.26?

```go
package main                          Code
import "fmt"                          3.26

func main() {

  var num int = -4

  switch num {

    case 0, 2, 4, 6, 8:
       fmt.Print("Even number")
       fmt.Print(num)

    case 1, 3, 5, 7, 9:
       fmt.Print("Odd number")
       fmt.Print(num)

    default:
       fmt.Println("Default")
  }
}
```

Chapter-4

Functions, Methods and Interfaces in Go Programming

Abstract: In this chapter, we explain functions and methods in Go programming. Go functions can return more than one value and this property is not available in many programming languages. Go methods are used with user defined data types such as structs. Go methods can be can be considered as a light form of classes of C++ language. Interfaces are data types, they involve the use of methods, and interfaces can also be considered as a technique of object oriented programming.

4.1 Functions

Functions are program units which can be executed many times. The syntax of Go function without return values and input parameters is as

```
func functionName() {

    // statements
}
```

In fact every go program contains at least one function which is the main function. A function can be called inside main function or inside other functions.

Example-4.1: In Code-4.1, we illustrate how to write a function and call it inside the main function.

```
package main                          Code
import ("fmt")                        4.1

func main() {
  myFunc() // function call
}
func myFunc() {

  fmt.Println("Inside myFunc!")
}
```

Output(s):
Inside myFunc!

4.2 Functions with Input Parameters

Functions can take input parameters. The syntax of a Go function with input parameters is as

```go
func functionName(varName1 dataType1, varName2 dataType2, ...) {

  // statements

}
```

Example-4.2: The function of Code-4.2 gets two input parameters; name and age.

```go
package main
import "fmt"

func main() {

  myFunc("Ilhan", 28)
  myFunc("Vera", 10)

}

func myFunc(name string, age int) {

  fmt.Println("Hello", name + ".", "You are ", age, " years old.")

}
```
Code 4.2

Output(s):
Hello Ilhan. You are 28 years old.
Hello Vera. You are 10 years old.

Example-4.3: Code-4.2 can be written as Code-4.3.

```go
package main
import "fmt"
import "strconv"

func main() {

  myFunc("Ilhan", 28)
  myFunc("Vera", 10)
}
```
Code 4.3

```go
func myFunc(name string, age int) {

    a := "Hello " + name + ". You are " + strconv.Itoa(age) + " years old."
    fmt.Println(a)
}
```

Output(s):
Hello Ilhan. You are 28 years old.
Hello Vera. You are 10 years old.

In Code-4.3, we used the package strconv where integer to string conversion function strconv.Itoa is available, and this function is used to convert integer values to strings.

4.3 Go Functions with Return Values

Go functions can return more than one value. The syntax of the Go function with return values is

```go
func funcName(var1 Type1, var2 Type2, ...) (r1 retType1, r2 retType2, ...) {

    // statements

    return r1, r2, ...
}
```

Example-4.4: In this example, we show how to define a function which gets two integers and returns the sum and difference of these two integers.

```go
package main                                          Code
import "fmt"                                           4.4

func myFunc(a int, b int) (sum int, diff int) {

    sum = a + b
    diff = a - b

    return sum, diff // or use just "return"
}

func main() {

    x := 12
    y := 23

    r1, r2 := myFunc(x, y)

    fmt.Println("Sum result is: ", r1)
    fmt.Println("Difference result is: ", r2)
}
```

73

Output(s):
Sum result is: 35
Difference result is: -11

The function in Code-4.4 can be written either as in Code-4.5 or as in Code-4.6.

```
func myFunc(a int, b int) (int, int) {          Code
                                                4.5
    sum := a + b
    diff := a - b

    return sum, diff
}
```

```
func myFunc(a int, b int) (sum int, diff int) {   Code
                                                  4.6
    sum = a + b
    diff = a - b

    return
}
```

4.4 Unused Returned Function Values

If some of the returned values of a function are not used, we use underscore, _, to omit these
retuned values.

Example-4.5: In Code-4.7, the first returned value is omitted using underscore.

```
package main                                   Code
import "fmt"                                    4.7

func myFunc(a int, b int) (sum int, diff int) {

    sum = a + b
    diff = a - b
    return sum, diff
}

func main() {

    x := 12
    y := 23

    _, r2 := myFunc(x, y)

    fmt.Println("Difference result is: ", r2)
}
```

Output(s):
Difference result is: -11

4.5 Anonymous Go Functions

Anonymous functions do not have a name, and they can be defined inside main function and can be called immediately inside main function whenever they are needed.

4.5.1 Declaring an Anonymous Function

An anonymous function is defined as

```
func () {

    // statements

}
```

4.5.2 Immediate Invocation of Anonymous Functions

An anonymous function can be invoked immediately at its definition using parentheses () as in

```
func () {

    // statements

} () // () is used to invoke the function
```

Example-4.6: The anonymous function can be immediately invoked when it is defined.

```
package main
import "fmt"

func main () {

    func () {

        fmt.Println ("Hello World!")

    } () // function is automatically invoked
}
```
Code 4.8

Output(s):
Hello World!

4.5.3 Immediate Invocation of Anonymous Functions with Arguments

An anonymous function with arguments can be invoked immediately at its definition as in

```
func(var1 Type1, var2 Type2, ...){

    // statements

}(value1, value2, ...)
```

Example-4.7: The anonymous function can be immediately invoked when it is defined.

```
package main                                          Code
import "fmt"                                           4.9

func main() {

  func(a int, b float32){

    fmt.Println("a = ", a)
    fmt.Println("b = ", b)

  }(4, 13.9) // function is automatically invoked

}
```

Output(s):
a = 4
b = 13.9!

4.5.4 Assigning Anonymous Function to a Variable

An anonymous function can be assigned to a variable and the variable can be used to call the function. An anonymous function is assigned to a variable as in

```
varName := func(){

    // statements

}
```

and the function is invoked using the variable name as

```
varName()
```

If the anonymous function have some arguments, i.e., we have

76

```
varName := func(var1 Type1, var2 Type2, ...){

    // statements

}
```

then the function is invoked using the variable name as

```
varName(value1, value2, ...)
```

Example-4.8: In this example, anonymous function is assigned to a variable, and the variable is used to invoke the function.

```
package main                            Code
import "fmt"                            4.10

func main() {

  v := func(){

    fmt.Println("Hello World!")

  }
  v() // invokes the function
}
```

Output(s):
Hello World!

Example-4.9: In this example, anonymous function with argument is assigned to a variable, and the variable is used to invoke the function, a value is sent to the function via variable.

```
package main                            Code
import "fmt"                            4.11

func main() {

  v := func(num int){

    fmt.Println("Number is:", num)

  }

  v(48) // invokes the function
}
```

Output(s):
Number is: 48

77

4.5.5 Passing Anonymous Functions as Arguments

Anonymous functions can be used as arguments of functions.

Example-4.10: In this example, an anonymous function is used for the argument of another anonymous function.

```
package main                                        Code
import "fmt"                                         4.12

func main() {

  myFnc1 := func(num1 int){

    fmt.Println("Number is:", num1)

  }

  myFnc2 := func(num2 int,  myFnc1 func(num1 int)){

    myFnc1(num2)

  }

  myFnc2(24, myFnc1)
}
```

Output(s):
Number is: 24

4.5.6 Variadic Functions in Golang

A variadic function is a function with a variable number of arguments. The syntax of variadic function is as

```
function funcName(param1, param2 ... dataType) dataType {

  // statements
}
```

Example-4.11: Assume that we declare a variadic function as

```
func myVarFunc(a int, b ...int) {

  // statements
}
```

If we call the function as

```
myVarFunc(1, 2, 3, 4)
```

then 1 is passed to a, and the integers 2, 3, and 4 are passed to b.

If we call the function as

$$myVarFunc(1)$$

then 1 is passed to a, and nothing is passed to b.

For different number of parameters of different types we can also use the variadic function prototype

```
func myVarFunc(a ...interface{}) {

    // statements
}
```

Example-4.12: In this example, we use a variadic function with integer arguments.

```
package main                              Code
import "fmt"                              4.12

func myVarFunc(a ... int) {

  for indx := range a {

    fmt.Printf("%v ", a[indx])
  }

  fmt.Println();
}
func main() {

  myVarFunc(23, 45)   // 2 arguments
  myVarFunc(-4, 63, 94, -34)   // 4 arguments
}
```

Output(s):

23 45
-4 63 94 -34

Example-4.13: In this example, we use a variadic function which takes different data types in its arguments.

```
package main                              Code
import "fmt"                              4.12

func main() {
  myVarFunc("Hello", "World!")
  myVarFunc("Hello", "Ilhan,", 35)
  myVarFunc(45, 67, "are numbers")
}
```

```go
func myVarFunc(arg ... interface{}) {

  for _, val := range arg {

    fmt.Printf("%v ", val)
  }

  fmt.Println();
}
```

Output(s):

Hello World!
Hello Ilhan, 35
45 67 are numbers

4.6 Methods in Go Programming

Go does not have classes as in C++. However, user defined data types and functions can be used together in methods. Thus, methods can be considered as light version of classes used in object oriented programming languages. Methods can be used with structs.

A method is declared as

```go
func (receiverName receiverType) methodName(arguments) returnType {

  // statements
}
```

where `receiverType` is usually a **struct** data type, and using the struct object-name, `receiverName,` the method can be called as

<code>receiverName.methodName(arg)</code>

and this is similar to OOP-like method call. And inside body of the method, receiver parameters can be accessed using the dot operator, i.e., `receiverName.parameter`

Example-4.14: In this example, we illustrate how to write a method which uses a struct data type as receiver. First, let's write the skeleton of the program as in Code-4.13 where we have declared a function with name myMethod.

```
package main                    Code
import "fmt"                    4.13

func myMethod() {

}

func main() {

}
```

In the second step, we declare a struct data type named person as in Code-4.14

```
package main                    Code
import "fmt"                    4.14

type person struct{

  name string
}


func myMethod() {

}

func main() {

}
```

In the third step, we declare a variable of the **struct person** in front of the function name in yellow as in Code-4.15. The new function structure in Code-4.15 is called a method in go.

```
package main                    Code
import "fmt"                    4.15

type person struct{

  name string
}

func (a person) myMethod() {

}

func main() {

}
```

The body of the method can access to the parameters of the struct object as in Code-4.16 where a.name is displayed using the printf() function.

```
package main                        Code
import "fmt"                        4.16

type person struct{

  name string
}


func (a person) myMethod() {

    fmt.Println("Hello", a.name)
}

func main() {


}
```

In the final step, we write the body of the main function as in Code-4.17 where we create a struct object with name b and use this object to call myMethod()

```
package main                        Code
import "fmt"                        4.17

type person struct{

  name string
}

func (a person) myMethod() {

    fmt.Println("Hello", a.name)
}

func main() {

  b := person{"Ilhan"}

  b.myMethod()
}
```

Output(s):
Hello Ilhan

82

Example-4.15: In this example, we calculate the area of a circle using a method.

```go
package main                                          Code
import "fmt"                                          4.18
import "math"

type myCircle struct {

  rd float32 // radius
}

func (a myCircle) getArea() float32 {

  return math.Pi * a.rd * a.rd // area calculation
}

func main() {

  b := myCircle{3.5}

  fmt.Println("The area of the circle:", b.getArea())
}
```

Output(s):
The area of the circle: 38.484512

Example-4.16: Two methods can be associated with the same structure.

```go
package main                                          Code
import "fmt"                                          4.19
import "math"

type myCircle struct {

  rd float32 // radius
}

func main() {

  b := myCircle{5.3}

  fmt.Println("The area of the circle:", b.getArea())
  fmt.Println("The perimeter of the circle:", b.getArea())
}

func (a myCircle) getArea() float32 {

  return math.Pi * a.rd * a.rd // area calculation
}
```

```go
func (a myCircle) getPerim() float32 {

    return 2 * math.Pi * a.rd // circumference calculation
}
```

Output(s):
The area of the circle: 88.247345
The perimeter of the circle: 88.247345

Example-4.17: In this example, we illustrate the use of a function and a method which give the same output.

```go
package main
import "fmt"

type employee struct {
  ID     int
  name   string
  salary float32
}

//this is normal function
func dispEmpInfo(m employee)  {

  fmt.Println("ID:", m.ID)
  fmt.Println("Name:", m.name)
  fmt.Println("Salary:", m.salary)
}

//this is a method
func (m employee) printEmpInfo()  {

  fmt.Println("ID:", m.ID)
  fmt.Println("Name:", m.name)
  fmt.Println("Salary:", m.salary,"\n")
}

func main() {

  e := employee{45678, "Ilhan Gazi", 5675}
  e.printEmpInfo() // call method
  dispEmpInfo(e) // call function
}
```

Code 4.20

Output(s):
ID: 45678
Name: Ilhan Gazi
Salary: 5675

ID: 45678
Name: Ilhan Gazi
Salary: 5675

4.6.1 Receiver Types

Receivers can be of two types which are value receivers and pointer receivers. The syntax for pointer use with go methods is as

```
func (ptr* dataType) methodName(arguments) dataType {

  //statements

}
```

Example-4.18: In this example, we use value receiver and pointer receiver for a method.

```
package main                          Code
import "fmt"                          4.21

type person struct{

  name string
}

func (a person) disp1() {

  fmt.Println("Hello", a.name)
}

func (a* person) disp2() {

  fmt.Println("Hello", a.name)
}

func main() {

  b := person{"Ilhan"}

  b.disp1()
  b.disp2()
}
```

Output(s):
Hello Ilhan
Hello Ilhan

Example-4.19: Pointer receiver can be used to change values of the object parameters.

```
package main                                        Code
import  "fmt"                                        4.22

type person struct{

  name string
}

func (a person) disp() {

  fmt.Println("Hello", a.name)
}

func (a* person) changeName(newName string) {

  a.name = newName
}

func main() {

  b := person{"Ilhan"}
  b.disp()

  b.changeName("Vera")
  b.disp()
}
```

Output(s):
Hello Ilhan
Hello Vera

4.6.2 Method with User Defined Data Types Other than Structs

Go methods can be written with any user defined data types, these data types can be structs or simple data types defined by the keyword **typedef**.

Example-4.20: In this example, we use a method with a user defined data type other than a struct.

```go
package main                                    Code
import "fmt"                                     4.23

type myData float32

func (num1 myData) mySum (num2 myData) myData {

  return num1 + num2
}

func main() {

  var a  myData = 34.4
  var b  myData = 56.8

  sm := a.mySum(b)

  fmt.Println("Summation result:", sm)
}
```

Output(s):
Summation result: 91.2

4.7 Interfaces in Go

An interface is an abstract definition of a set of functions, and the implementations of these functions are usually associated with one or a number of user defined struct data types. It can be considered as a form of polymorphism in object oriented programming. The syntax of the interface declaration is as

```go
type interfaceName interface{

  methodName1 [return dataType]
  methodName2 [return dataType]
  methodName3 [return dataType]
         . . .
}
```

where method names with their return data types are also called method signatures.

87

Functions, Methods XE "Methods" and Interfaces XE "Interfaces" in Go Programming4.7 Interfaces XE "Interfaces" in Go

We can declare an interface variable as

```
var varName interface { /* method signatures */ }
```

Example-4.21: In this example, we declare interfaces using different methods.

```
package main                                                    Code
import "fmt"                                                     4.24

type geometricFunctions interface {
  getArea() float64
  getPerim() float64
}

func main() {

  var a geometricFunctions

  var b interface {}

  var c interface {myMethod1() float64; myMethod2() float64}

  fmt.Printf("Value of the interface variable a: %v\n", a)
  fmt.Printf("Type of the interface a is: %T \n\n", a)

  fmt.Printf("Value of the interface variable b: %v\n", b)
  fmt.Printf("Type of the interface b is: %T \n\n", b)

  fmt.Printf("Value of the interface variable c: %v\n", c)
  fmt.Printf("Type of the interface c is: %T \n\n", c)

  fmt.Printf("Value of the interface variable d: %v\n", c)
  fmt.Printf("Type of the interface d is: %T \n\n", c)
}
```

Output(s):
Value of the interface variable a: <nil>
Type of the interface a is: <nil>

Value of the interface variable b: <nil>
Type of the interface b is: <nil>

Value of the interface variable c: <nil>
Type of the interface c is: <nil>

Value of the interface variable d: <nil>
Type of the interface d is: <nil>

Example-4.22: In this example, we will illustrate how to write an interface and use it for struct objects. First, let's declare struct data type Code-4.25

```
package main                              Code
import "fmt"                              4.25

type myRectangle struct {

  width, height float64
}
```

In the second step, we implement two methods for this struct as in Code-4.26.

```
package main                              Code
import "fmt"                              4.26

type myRectangle struct {

  width, height float64
}

func (r myRectangle) getArea() float64 {

  return r.width * r.height
}

func (r myRectangle) getPerim() float64 {

  return 2 * (r.width + r.height)
}
```

In the second step, we write the main part of the program. For this purpose, we first declare the interface variable as in Code-4.27.

```
func main() {                             Code
                                          4.27
  var g interface { }

}
```

Next, we write the method names and return values of struct, i.e., method signatures, inside the interface as in Code-4.28.

```go
func main() {                                              Code
                                                           4.28
  var g interface {

    getArea() float64
    getPerim() float64

  }
}
```

In the next step, we initialize the interface variable as in Code-4.29.

```go
func main() {                                              Code
                                                           4.29
  var g interface {

    getArea() float64
    getPerim() float64

  } = myRectangle{width: 5, height: 12}

}
```

The interface variable g in Code-4.29 can access to the methods of the struct. Finally, we add Println() function to the program as in Code-4.30

```go
func main() {                                              Code
                                                           4.30
  var g interface {

    getArea() float64
    getPerim() float64

  } = myRectangle{width: 5, height: 12}

  fmt.Println("Rectangle structure variable g:", g)

  fmt.Println("Rectangle area", g.getArea())

  fmt.Println("Rectangle perimeter", g.getPerim())
}
```

If we combine the program units, we get the entire program as in Code-4.31.

```
package main
import "fmt"

type myRectangle struct {

  width, height float64
}

func (r myRectangle) getArea() float64 {

  return r.width * r.height
}

func (r myRectangle) getPerim() float64 {

  return 2*(r.width + r.height)
}

func main() {

  var g interface {

    getArea() float64
    getPerim() float64

  } = myRectangle{width: 5, height: 12}

  fmt.Println("Rectangle structure variable g:", g)

  fmt.Println("Rectangle area", g.getArea())
  fmt.Println("Rectangle perimeter", g.getPerim())
}
```

Code 4.31

Output(s):
Rectangle structure variable g: {5 12}
Rectangle area 60
Rectangle perimeter 34

Example-4.23: We can write the Code-4.31 in a different manner. For this purpose, we can declare the interface using the keyword **type** as in Code-4.32.

```
type geometricFunctions interface {

  getArea() float64
  getPerim() float64
}
```

Code 4.32

Using the interface declaration in Code-4.32, we can write the entire program as in Code-4.33 where yellow part is the alternative form of interface variable declaration compared to Code-4.31.

```
package main                                              Code
import "fmt"                                              4.33

type geometricFunctions interface {

  getArea() float64
  getPerim() float64
}

type myRectangle struct {

  width, height float64
}

func (r myRectangle) getArea() float64 {

  return r.width * r.height
}

func (r myRectangle) getPerim() float64 {

  return 2*(r.width + r.height)
}

func main() {

  var g geometricFunctions = myRectangle{width: 5, height: 12}

  fmt.Println("Rectangle structure variable g:", g)

  fmt.Println("Rectangle area", g.getArea())
  fmt.Println("Rectangle perimeter", g.getPerim())
}
```

When Code-4.33 is run, we get the outputs
Rectangle structure variable g: {5 12}
Rectangle area 60
Rectangle perimeter 34

92

Example-4.24: Interfaces are data types and as for any data types, we can define arrays for interfaces. In this example, we illustrate how to declare an array of interfaces. The yellow part in Code-4.34 is the interface data type.

```go
package main
import "fmt"

type myCar struct {
  name string
}

type myJob struct {
  name string
}

func (c myCar) getName() string {

  return c.name
}

func (j myJob) getName() string {

  return j.name
}

func main() {

  a :=  myCar{"BMW"}
  b :=  myJob{"Engineer"}

  // var arrayName = [length]dataType{val1, val2, ...}
  var g = [2] interface { getName() string } {a, b}

  fmt.Println("g:", g)

  fmt.Printf("g[0] value: %v \n", g[0].getName())

  fmt.Printf("g[1] value: %v", g[1].getName())
}
```

Code 4.34

Output(s):
g: [{BMW} {Engineer}]
g[0] value: BMW
g[1] value: Engineer

Example-4.25: In Example-4.24, we illustrate how to declare an interface and use it with a struct data type. In this example, we will extend Example-4.24. The interface data type can be used with more than one struct data type. In Code-4.35, we declare two more structs and implement the methods differently for different struct data types.

```
package main                                          Code
import "fmt"                                          4.35
import "math"

type geometricFunctions interface {
  getArea() float64
  getPerim() float64
}
type myRectangle struct {
  width, height float64
}
type myCircle struct {
  radius float64
}
type myTriangle struct {
  side1, side2, side3 float64
  height float64 // height for side1
}
func (r myRectangle) getArea() float64 {
  return r.width * r.height
}
func (r myRectangle) getPerim() float64 {
  return 2*(r.width + r.height)
}
func (c myCircle) getArea() float64 {
  return math.Pi * c.radius * c.radius
}
func (c myCircle) getPerim() float64 {
  return 2 * math.Pi * c.radius
}
func (t myTriangle) getArea() float64 {
  return t.side1 * t.height * 0.5
}
func (t myTriangle) getPerim() float64 {
  return (t.side1 + t.side2 + t.side3)
}
```

We can write the main function as in Code-4.36 where we used a function to display the parameters of different structs.

```
func disp(g geometricFunctions) {                    Code
                                                     4.36
  fmt.Println("Structure variable g:", g)
  fmt.Println("Area:", g.getArea())
  fmt.Println("Perimeter:", g.getPerim())
}
func main() {

  r := myRectangle{width: 5, height: 12}
  c := myCircle{radius: 5}
```

```
t := myTriangle{side1: 12, side2: 10, side3: 10, height: 8}

disp(r)
disp(c)
disp(t)
}
```

When the Codes-4.35 and 4.36 are concatenated and run we get the outputs

Structure variable g: {5 12}
Area: 60
Perimeter: 34

Structure variable g: {5}
Area: 78.53981633974483
Perimeter: 31.41592653589793

Structure variable g: {12 10 10 8}
Area: 48
Perimeter: 32

4.7.1 Interfaces with Ordinary Data Types

Empty interfaces can be used with standard data types such as int, string, etc.

Example-4.26: In this example, we use empty interfaces having standard data values.

```
package main                                                    Code
import "fmt"                                                     4.37

func main() {

  var a interface { } = "Hello World!"
  var b interface { } = 45.6

  fmt.Printf("Value of the interface variable a: %v\n", a)
  fmt.Printf("Type of the interface a is: %T \n", a)

  fmt.Printf("Value of the interface variable a: %v\n", b)
  fmt.Printf("Type of the interface a is: %T \n", b)
}
```

Output(s):
Value of the interface variable a: Hello World!
Type of the interface a is: string
Value of the interface variable a: 45.6
Type of the interface a is: float64

4.7.2 Type Assertions for Interface

If a is an interface variable, then the expression

$$value, ok := a.(T)$$

returns the value of the interface, and ok is true if the value data type is T, otherwise if ok is false, no value is returned.

Example-4.27: This example illustrates the use of the type assertion.

```
package main                                              Code
import "fmt"                                              4.38

func main() {

  var a interface { } = 45.6
  value, ok := a.(float64)

  fmt.Printf("Value of the interface variable: %v\n", value)
  fmt.Printf("Assertion result: %v\n", ok)
}
```

Output(s):
Value of the interface variable: 45.6
Assertion result: true

Example-4.28: Type assertion can be used with struct data types.

```
package main                                              Code
import "fmt"                                              4.39

func main() {

  type person struct {

    name string
  }
  var a interface { } = person{"Ilhan"}
  value, ok := a.(person)

  fmt.Printf("Value of the interface variable: %v\n", value)
  fmt.Printf("Assertion result: %v\n", ok)
}
```

Output(s):
Value of the interface variable: {Ilhan}
Assertion result: true

Problems

1) Declare a function which prints "Hello Your-Name" to the screen, and call the function from the main() function.

2) Write a function which adds three integers and return the result to the calling function.

3) What is the output of the Code-4.40?

```
package main                                           Code
import "fmt"                                            4.40

func mySwap(a int, b int) {

  var t int = 0

  t = a
  a = b
  b = t
}

func main() {

  var num1 int = 56
  var num2 int = 78

  fmt.Println("Before swapping, numbers are: ", num1, num2)
  mySwap(num1, num2)
  fmt.Println("After swapping, numbers are: ", num1, num2)
}
```

4) What is the output of the Code-4.41?

```
package main                                           Code
import "fmt"                                            4.41

func mySwap(a* int, b* int) {
  var t int = 0
  t = *a
  *a = *b
  *b = t
}

func main() {

  var num1 int = 56
  var num2 int = 78

  fmt.Println("Before swapping, numbers are: ", num1, num2)
  mySwap(&num1, &num2)
  fmt.Println("After swapping, numbers are: ", num1, num2)
}
```

5) Write Code-4.40 using an anonymous function.

6) Write a function which gets three integers a, b, c from calling function, and the function returns c, b, a.

7) Write a function which gets an array from the calling function, and reverses the elements of the array and returns it.

8) Write a variadic function which gets a number of integers and retuns the product of these integers.

9) Write a variadic function which gets an integer, a string, and a real number, and the function just prints these values to the screen.

10) What is the main difference between a function and a method?

11) Define a struct for a circle, and write a method which calculates the circumference of the circle for the declared struct.

12) For the Code-4.42, declare an interface variable and call the methods in Code-4.42 using interface variable.

```
package main
import "fmt"

                                        Code
                                        4.42

type myNums struct {

  a, b float64
}

func (n myNums) myMethod1() float64 {

  return n.a * n.b + n.a
}

func (n myNums) myMethod2) float64 {

  return 2 * n.a + 3 * n.b
}
```

13) What is the output of the Code-4.43?

```
package main                                    Code
import "fmt"                                     4.43

func myRecFunc(a int) int {

  if a == 0 {

    return a

  } else {

    fmt.Printf("%d ", a)

    }

  a = a - 1
  return myRecFunc(a)
}

func main() {

  myRecFunc(5)
}
```

Chapter-5

Go Structures

Abstract: In this chapter, we explain structures in Go programming. A Structure is a data type which contains a number of different data types. That is, a structure can be considered as a group of data types. Structures can be used as records holding information about a person, a device, an event, etc.

5.1 Structures

Structures are declared using the keyword struct. A structure is used to collect a number of different data types into a single data type. Arrays elements belong to the same data whereas structure members can be of different data types.

The syntax of structure declaration in Go is as

```
type structName struct {

  var1 dataType1
  var2 dataType2
  var3 dataType3
       . . .
}
```

Once we have a structure data type; a variable, i.e., object, for this structure is defined as

```
var varName structName
```

The structure members of the variable varName can be initialized as

```
varName.var1 = val1; varName.var2 = val2; ...
```

The structure members of the variable varName can be initialized at the declaration as

```
var varName = structName { var1 : val1, var2 : val2, ...}
```

or as in

```
var varName = structName { val1,val2, ...}
```

Example-5.1: In this example, we declare a structure and define a structure variable and initialize variable members.

```
package main                                              Code
import "fmt"                                               5.1

type Student struct {

  student_name string

  student_num int

}

func main() {

  var st Student

  st.student_name = "Ilhan"

  st.student_num = 345678

  fmt.Println("Student name is:", st.student_name)

  fmt.Println("Student number is:", st.student_num)
}
```

Output(s):
Student name is: Ilhan
Student number is: 345678

Example-5.2:

```
package main                                              Code
import "fmt"                                               5.2

type Student struct {

  student_name string

  student_num int

}
```

```go
func main() {

  var st = Student {student_name :"Ilhan" , student_num : 345678}

  fmt.Println("Student name is:", st.student_name)

  fmt.Println("Student number is:", st.student_num)
}
```

Output(s):
Student name is: Ilhan
Student number is: 345678

The structure variable in Code-5.2 can also be initialized as

```go
var st = Student {"Ilhan", 345678}
```

Example-5.3: We can use Println() function to print structure members.

```go
package main                                              Code
import "fmt"                                               5.3

type Student struct {

  student_name string

  student_num int

  department string

}

func main() {

  var st = Student {"Ilhan", 345678, "Computer"}

  fmt.Println(st)

}
```

Output(s):

{Ilhan 345678 Computer}

Example-5.4: In this example we use := operator for a structure variable declaration.

```
package main                                              Code
import "fmt"                                              5.4

type Car struct {

  car_model string

  car_color string

  production_year uint

}

func main() {

  car1 := Car {"BMW", "Blue", 2020}

  fmt.Println(car1)

  fmt.Println("Car Model: ", car1.car_model)
  fmt.Println("Car Color: ", car1.car_color)
  fmt.Println("Car Year: ", car1.production_year)
}
```

Output(s):

{BMW Blue 2020}
Car Model: BMW
Car Color: Blue
Car Year: 2020

5.2 Structure Declaration Using the new Keyword

The new keyword can be used to declare a struct. Once declaration is complete, the dot notation can be used to initialize the struct variable.

Example-5.5: In this example, we illustrate how to use the **new** keyword to declare a struct.

```
package main                         Code
import "fmt"                         5.5

type Car struct {

  car_model string
  car_color string
  production_year uint
}
```

```go
func main() {

  var car1 = new(Car)

  car1.car_model = "BMW"
  car1.car_color = "Blue"
  car1.production_year = 2020

  fmt.Println(car1)
}
```

Output(s):

&{BMW Blue 2020}

5.3 Structure Declaration Using Pointer Address Operator

A struct can be declared using the pointer address operator(&).

Example-5.6:

```go
package main                              Code
import "fmt"                              5.6

type Car struct {

  car_model string
  car_color string
  production_year uint
}

func main() {

  var car1 = &Car{"BMW", "Blue", 2020}

  fmt.Println(car1)
}
```

Output(s):

&{BMW Blue 2020}

5.4 Types of Structs in Go

There are two types of structs in Go which are

```
named struct
anonymous struct
```

5.4.1 Named Structs

We have already used named structs in previous sections.

5.4.2 Anonymous Structs

These structs do not have a name. They are usually assigned to variables to be used.

Example-5.7: In this example, we declare, initialize and print an anonymous struct.

```
package main                           Code
import "fmt"                            5.7


func main() {

  student := struct {

  name string
  id_number int

  } { "Ilhan", 456789 }

  fmt.Println(student)
}
```

Output(s):

{Ilhan 456789}

5.4.3 Anonymous Fields in a Struct

In anonymous fields only data types are declared, member names are not available.

Example-5.8:

```
package main                              Code
import "fmt"                              5.8

func main() {

  type Student struct {

    string
    int
  }

  var st Student

  st.string = "Ilhan"
  st.int = 345678

  fmt.Println(st)
}
```

Output(s):

{Ilhan 345678}

Example-5.9: The Code-5.8 of the previous example can be written as Code-5.9.

```
package main                              Code
import "fmt"                              5.9

func main() {

  type Student struct {

    string
    int
  }

  var st = Student { "Ilhan", 345678}

  fmt.Println(st)
}
```

Output(s):

{Ilhan 345678}

We can use the keyword **new** and address operator **&** to created anonymous struct variables.

5.5 Functions as Struct Members

Functions can be used as members of structs.

Example-5.10: Let's use a function as a member of a struct. For this purpose, let's declare a struct as in Code-5.10.

```
package main                                          Code
import "fmt"                                          5.10

func main() {

  type Student struct {

    name string
  }
}
```

We declare a function type using the keyword **type**, and introduce a new member of the struct as in Code-5.11.

```
package main                                          Code
import "fmt"                                          5.11

type myFunc func() (string)  // declare function type

func main() {

  type Student struct {

    name string
    structFunc myFunc  // new member
  }
}
```

We define a variable of the struct as in Code-5.12 where members of the variable are not initialized yet.

```
package main                                          Code
import "fmt"                                          5.12

type myFunc func() (string)  // declare function type

func main() {

  type Student struct {
    name string
    structFunc myFunc  // declare function
  }
```

```go
    var st =  Student{

        name:

        structFunc:
    }

}
```

In Code-5.13, members of the variable are initialized and the function member is called in Println function.

```go
package main                                          Code
import "fmt"                                           5.13

type myFunc func() (string)  // declare function type

func main() {

  type Student struct {

    name string
    structFunc myFunc   // declare function
  }

   var st =  Student{

        name: "Ilhan",

        structFunc: func() string { // declare function body

            return "Hello World!"
        },
  }

  fmt.Println(st.structFunc())
}
```

5.6 Comparing and Assigning Struct Variables

Struct variables can be compared to each other, and one can be assigned to the other if they belong to the same struct type.

Example-5.11: In this example, two struct variables are compared to each other.

```go
package main                                    Code
import "fmt"                                     5.14

type Student struct {

    name string
    id_number int
  }

func main() {

  var st1 =  Student {"Ilhan", 456789}
  var st2 =  Student {"Ilhan", 456789}

  if(st1 == st2) {
    fmt.Println("Variables are equal")

  } else {
    fmt.Println("Variables are not equal")
  }
}
```

Output(s): Variables are equal

Example-5.12: In this example, we assign a struct variable to another one.

```go
package main                                    Code
import "fmt"                                     5.15

type Student struct {

    name string
    id_number int
  }

func main() {

  var st1 =  Student {"Ilhan", 456789}
  var st2 =  Student { }

  st2 = st1

  fmt.Println(st2)
}
```

Output(s): {Ilhan 456789}

Problems

1) Declare a structure which has two members, one of them is of integer type and the other is of floating point type. Define a structure variable and initialize its members.

2) What are the mistakes in Code-5.16?

```
package main                                          Code
import "fmt"                                          5.16

  Student struct {

  student_name string

  student_num integer

}

func main() {

  var st = Student {student_name ::"Ilhan" , student_num :: 345678}

  fmt.Println("Student name is:"; st.student_name)

  fmt.Println("Student number is:"; st.student_num)
}
```

3) Define a variable for the structure in Code-5.17 and initialize its members.

```
type Student struct {          Code
                               5.17
    student_name string

    student_num int

    department string
}
```

4) The main() function of a go program is written as in Code-5.18. The program contains a structure declaration which is missing in the program. Declare the structure and write the rest of the program.

```go
func main() {                                    Code
                                                 5.18
  car1 := Car {"Ford", "White", 2023}

  fmt.Println(car1)

  fmt.Println("Car Model: ", car1.car_model)
  fmt.Println("Car Color: ", car1.car_color)
  fmt.Println("Car Year: ", car1.production_year)
}
```

5) Fill the missing parts in Code-5.19 according to your will.

```go
package main                          Code
import "fmt"                          5.19

type Car struct {

  car_model string
  car_color string
  age ...
}

func main() {

  var car1 = new ...

  car1.car_model = ...
  car1...
  car1....

  fmt.Println(car1)
}
```

Chapter-6

Go Loops

Abstract: In this chapter, we explain loops in Go programming. Contrary to many programming languages, there is only for-loop in go programming. In fact, we can implement while-loop and do-while loop using for-loop. Loops are vital parts of every programming language to perform iterative processes. Go provides range keyword which makes it easy to perform iterations using for loops. We also cover break and continue statements.

6.1 For-Loop

The syntax of the for-loop is as

```
for initialization; loopCondition; update {

    // statements

}
```

Example-6.1: In Code-6.1, we illustrate the use of the for-loop.

```
package main                              Code
                                           6.1
import "fmt"

func main() {

  fmt.Println("Before Loop \n")

  for indx := 0; indx < 3; indx++ {

    fmt.Printf("Inside Loop, ")
    fmt.Println("indx =", indx)

  }

  fmt.Println("\nAfter Loop")
}
```

Output(s):
Before Loop

Inside Loop, indx = 0
Inside Loop, indx = 1
Inside Loop, indx = 2

After Loop

Example-6.2: In this example, the update part of the for-loop uses indx += 5

```
package main                                    Code
                                                6.2
import "fmt"

func main() {

    for indx := 0; indx <= 25; indx += 5 {

        fmt.Printf("Inside Loop, ")

        fmt.Println("indx =", indx)

    }

}
```

Output(s):
Inside Loop, indx = 0
Inside Loop, indx = 5
Inside Loop, indx = 10
Inside Loop, indx = 15
Inside Loop, indx = 20
Inside Loop, indx = 25

6.1.1 The Infinite for-loop

Infinite loop can be created using either the syntax

```
for {

    // infinite loop

}
```

or the syntax

```go
for true {

  // infinite loop

}
```

Example-6.3: In this example, an infinite loop is written using for-loop structure.

```go
package main                              Code
                                          6.3
import "fmt"

func main() {

  for {

    fmt.Println("Hello World !")

  }

}
```

Output(s):
Hello World !
Hello World !
Hello World !
Hello World !
　...
　...

6.1.2 Go Range

We can use the keyword **range** in a for-loop to process the elements of array, string, or map.

The keyword **range** is used with a for loop as

```go
for index, item := range myArray {

  // statements

}
```

where myArray is an array, index, and item are the element-index and element value of array element. That is, **range** keyword returns two values of an array element, and these are the index and value of the array element.

Example-6.4: In this example, we define an integer array with five elements and use it with a for-loop using the keyword range.

```
package main                                          Code
import "fmt"                                           6.4

func main() {

  myArray := [5] int {2, 4, 6, 8, 10}

  for index, item := range myArray {

    fmt.Printf("index = %d, item = %d \n", index, item)

  }
}
```

Output(s):
index = 0, item = 2
index = 1, item = 4
index = 2, item = 6
index = 3, item = 8
index = 4, item = 10

The range keyword returns the current index and the current value of the array element. If the current value is the only thing to be used, then the index can be ignored using the blank identifier.

Example-6.5: In this example, we omit the index value returned by the range keyword.

```
package main                                       Code
import "fmt"                                        6.5

func main() {

  var myArray = [] int {2, 4, 6, 8, 10}

  for _, item := range myArray {

    fmt.Printf("item = %d \n",  item)

  }

}
```

Output(s):
item = 2
item = 4

item = 6
item = 8
item = 10

Example-6.6: Another for-loop with the **range** keyword.

```
package main                                          Code
import ("fmt")                                         6.6

func main() {

   numbers := [4] string{"zero", "one", "two", "three"}

   for indx, value := range numbers {

      fmt.Printf("%d  %s \n", indx, value)

   }
}
```

Output(s):
0 zero
1 one
2 two
3 three

6.1.3 The Conditional for-loop

The conditional for-loop contains Boolean expression after **for** keyword, and as long as the condition is true loop body is executed.

Example-6.7: In this example, we use a conditional expression in for-loop structure.

```
package main                        Code
import "fmt"                         6.7

func main() {

  var indx int = 0

  for indx < 8 {

     fmt.Println("indx = ", indx)

     indx += 2
  }

}
```

Output(s):
indx = 0
indx = 2
indx = 4
indx = 6

6.1.4 The for-loop with Map

A for-loop can be written with the **map** data type.

Example-6.8: In this example, we use for-loop with the **map** data type.

```go
package main
import "fmt"

func main() {

  var numbers = map[int] float32 {

    2: 3.45,
    4: 5.78,
    6: 7.93,
  }

  for indx, value := range numbers {

    fmt.Printf("indx = %v, value = %v \n", indx, value)

  }
}
```

Code 6.8

Output(s):
indx = 2, value = 3.45
indx = 4, value = 5.78
indx = 6, value = 7.93

6.1.5 The Nested-for loop

Two or more for-loops can be used in a nested manner.

Example-6.9: In this example, we use two for-loops in a nested manner.

```
package main                                                    Code
import "fmt"                                                     6.9

func main() {

  for indxN := 0; indxN < 3; indxN++ {

    for indxM := 0; indxM < 3; indxM++ {

      fmt.Printf("indxN = %v, indxM = %v \n", indxN, indxM)

    }

    fmt.Println("Quitted inner loop\n");

  }

  fmt.Println("Quitted outer loop\n");

}
```

Output(s):

indxN = 0, indxM = 0
indxN = 0, indxM = 1
indxN = 0, indxM = 2
Quitted inner loop

indxN = 1, indxM = 0
indxN = 1, indxM = 1
indxN = 1, indxM = 2
Quitted inner loop

indxN = 2, indxM = 0
indxN = 2, indxM = 1
indxN = 2, indxM = 2
Quitted inner loop

Quitted outer loop

6.1.6 The Continue Statement

When the keyword **continue** is met, the statements below the keyword **continue** is skipped and program execution goes to the beginning of the loop.

Example-6.10: In this example, we illustrate the use of the **continue** statement.

```go
package main
import ("fmt")

func main() {

  var indx int

  for indx = 0; indx < 8; indx +=2 {

    if indx == 4 {
      fmt.Println("indx =", indx, "is skipped")

      continue

      fmt.Println("This line is not executed")
    }

    fmt.Println("indx =", indx)
  }
}
```
Code
6.10

Output(s):
indx = 0
indx = 2
indx = 4 is skipped
indx = 6

6.1.7 Strings with For-Loop

Strings can be considered as character arrays. We can use for-loop with a string.

Example-6.11: In this example, we illustrate the use of the for-loop with a string.

```go
package main
import ("fmt")

func main() {

  msg := "Hello World!"

  for indx := 0; indx < len(msg); indx++ {

    fmt.Printf("%c\t", msg[indx])
  }
}
```
Code
6.11

Output(s):
H   e   l   l   o   W   o   r   l   d   !

6.1.8 The Break Statement in For-Loop

The **break** keyword is used to terminate the loop execution. Usually a condition is checked before the break statement, and upon the occurrence of the condition the loop is terminated by the break statement.

Example-6.12: This example illustrates the use of the break statement in a for-loop.

```
package main                                          Code
import ("fmt")                                        6.12

func main() {

  var indx int

  for indx = 0; indx < 8; indx +=2 {

    if indx == 4 {

      fmt.Printf("Before the break statement, indx = %d \n", indx)
      fmt.Printf("The program is terminated")

      break
    }

    fmt.Println("indx =", indx)
  }
}
```

Output(s):
indx = 0
indx = 2
Before the break statement, indx = 4
The program is terminated

6.1.9 Do-While Loop Implementation with For-Loop

A do-while loop can be implemented using a for-loop structure as in

```
for {

  // statements

  if !booleanCondition {
      break
  }

}
```

120

6.1.10 Goto Statement in For-Loop

The goto statement can be used either as

```
label: // statements
  ...
  ...
goto label
```

or as

```
goto label
  ...
  ...
label: // statements
```

We can use goto statement with for-loop.

Example-6.13: In this example, we use goto statement is a for-loop.

```
package main                                    Code
import ("fmt")                                   6.13

func main() {

  var indx int

  for indx = 0; indx < 8; indx +=2 {
    fmt.Println("Inside the loop, indx =", indx)

    if indx == 4 {

      goto quit_loop
    }
  }
  quit_loop:

  fmt.Println("\nLoop is quitted")
  fmt.Println("indx =", indx)
}
```

Output(s):
Inside the loop, indx = 0
Inside the loop, indx = 2
Inside the loop, indx = 4

Loop is quitted
indx = 4

6.1.11 For Channel

A for loop can iterate over the sequential values sent on the channel until it is closed.

Example-6.14:

```
package main                              Code
import "fmt"                              6.14

func main() {

  ch := make(chan int)

  go func() {
     ch <- 1
     ch <- 2
     ch <- 3
     ch <- 4
     close(ch)
  }()

  for indx:= range ch {
     fmt.Printf("indx = %v \n", indx)
  }
}
```

Output(s):

indx = 1
indx = 2
indx = 3
indx = 4

Problems

1) Write a program which displays the first 12 odd integers. Use for-loop in your code.

2) Write a Go program which gets an integer from the user and calculates the factorial of the entered number.

3) Write a program which calculates and display the sum of the series

$$1 + \frac{1}{5} + \left(\frac{1}{5}\right)^2 + \left(\frac{1}{5}\right)^3 + \dots$$

4) Write three separate Go programs which display the patterns in Figure-6.8.

Figure-6.8 Patterns to be displayed.

6) Write a Go program that inputs an integer from the user determines the number of digits in the entered number.

7) Write a C which converts a binary number to decimal.

8) Write a Go program which gets two integer numbers from the user and calculates the highest common factor and then print the result to the screen.

9) Write a Go program which performs the multiplication of two integers using a for-loop and addition operator, i.e., + operator.

Chapter-7

Arrays in Go

Abstract: In this chapter, we explain arrays in Go programming. Arrays are used to hold a number of values of the same type. Arrays can be considered as the light version of data structures. This chapter covers arrays in details, we explain the subjects; how to define arrays, how to process the elements of an array, array initialization, copying arrays and passing an array to a function argument etc.

7.1 Arrays

An array can be considered as a number of variables belonging to the same data type. Thus, an array stores a number of values with the same data type.

In go programming, an array can be declared either using **var** keyword or using := assignment symbol. Besides, in array declarations, the size of the array can be specified or it can be determined by the compiler if it is not written.

7.1.1 Syntaxes for Array Declaration

Using **var** keyword:

```
var arrayName = [length]dataType{val1, val2, ...} //length is written

or

var arrayName = [...]dataType{val1, val2, ...} // length is determined
                                               // by the compiler
```

Using := assignment symbol:

```
arrayName := [length]dataType{val1, val2, ...} //length is written

or

arrayName := [...]dataType{val1, val2, ...} // length is determined
                                            // by the compiler
```

Example-7.1: In this example, we declare arrays using the keyword **var**.

```
package main                                    Code
import ("fmt")                                   7.1

func main() {

  var a1 = [3] int {1, 2, 3}

  var a2 = [...] float32 {2.4, 5.6, 0.34, 12.1}

  fmt.Println(a1)

  fmt.Println(a2)

}
```

Output(s):
[1 2 3]
[2.4 5.6 0.34 12.1]

Example-7.2: In this example, we declare arrays using := assignment symbol.

```
package main                                    Code
import ("fmt")                                   7.2

func main() {

  a1 := [3] int {5, 8, 43}

  a2 := [...] string {"Apple", "Banana", "Orange"}

  fmt.Println(a1)

  fmt.Println(a2)

}
```

Output(s):
[5 8 43]
[Apple Banana Orange]

7.2 Accessing Array Elements

Array indexes start with 0. If a is an array, then a[0] refers to the first element, and a[1] refers to the second element of array a.

Example-7.3: In this example, we show how to access to an array elements.

```
package main                                      Code
import ("fmt")                                     7.3

func main() {

  numbers := [4] int {45, 78, 98, 67}

  fmt.Println("numbers[0] -->", numbers[0])

  fmt.Println("numbers[1] -->", numbers[1])

  fmt.Println("numbers[2] -->", numbers[2])
}
```

Output(s):

numbers[0] --> 45

numbers[1] --> 78

numbers[2] --> 98

Example-7.4: In this example, we illustrate how to change elements of an array.

```
package main                                      Code
import ("fmt")                                     7.4

func main() {

  numbers := [4] int {45, 78, 98, 67}
  numbers [0] = 10; numbers [1] = 24

  fmt.Println("numbers[0] -->", numbers[0])

  fmt.Println("numbers[1] -->", numbers[1])

  fmt.Println("numbers[2] -->", numbers[2])
}
```

Output(s):
numbers[0] --> 10
numbers[1] --> 24
numbers[2] --> 98

7.3 Array Initialization

Arrays can be initialized when they are declared. Default initialization value for number arrays is 0, and it is "" for strings

Example-7.5: In this example, we initialize only some elements of the arrays.

```
package main                                    Code
import ("fmt")                                   7.5

func main() {

    a1 := [5] int {}
    a2 := [5] int {12, 78}
    a3 := [5] float32 {3.4, 7.9}
    a4 := [5] string {"Apple", "Banana"}

    fmt.Println(a1)
    fmt.Println(a2)
    fmt.Println(a3)
    fmt.Println(a4)
}
```

Output(s):
[0 0 0 0 0]
[12 78 0 0 0]
[3.4 7.9 0 0 0]
[Apple Banana   ]

7.4 Initialization of Specific Array Elements

Some of the array elements can be initialized by referring to their indexes.

Example-7.6: In this example, second and seventh elements of an array are initialized.

```
package main                                    Code
import ("fmt")                                   7.6

func main() {

    a := [8] float32 {1 : 3.4, 6 : 7.9}

    fmt.Println(a)
}
```

Output(s):
[0 3.4 0 0 0 0 7.9 0]

127

7.5 Length of an Array

The length of an array can be found using the len() function.

Example-7.7: In this example, we calculate and display length of some arrays.

```
package main                                              Code
import ("fmt")                                            7.7

func main() {

    a1 := [5] int {}
    a2 := [8] int {12, 78}
    a3 := [15] string {"Apple", "Banana"}

    fmt.Println("Length of array a1 is:", len(a1))
    fmt.Println("Length of array a2 is:", len(a2))
    fmt.Println("Length of array a3 is:", len(a3))
}
```

Output(s):
Length of array a1 is: 5
Length of array a2 is: 8
Length of array a3 is: 15

7.6 Multi-Dimensional Arrays

Multi-dimensional arrays are defined either as

```
var arrayName = [Length1][Length2]..[LengthN] dataType {...}
```

or as

```
arrayName := [Length1][Length2]..[LengthN] dataType {...}
```

Example-7.8: In this example, we declare a two dimensional array and access to its elements.

```
package main                                              Code
import ("fmt")                                            7.8

func main() {

    a := [2][3] int { {1, 2, 3 }, {4, 5, 6} }

    fmt.Println("a = ", a)

    fmt.Println("a[0] = ", a[0])
    fmt.Println("a[1] = ", a[1])
```

```
fmt.Println("a[0][2] = ", a[0][2])

fmt.Println("Length of a is:", len(a))

}
```

Output(s):

a = [[1 2 3] [4 5 6]]

a[0] = [1 2 3]

a[1] = [4 5 6]

a[0][2] = 3

Length of a is: 2

Example-7.9: In this example, we initialize the array elements one by one.

```
package main                          Code
import ("fmt")                        7.9

func main() {

  var a [2][3] int

  a[0][0] = 1
  a[0][1] = 2
  a[0][2] = 3

  a[1][0] = 4
  a[1][1] = 5
  a[1][2] = 6

  fmt.Println("a = ", a)
}
```

Output(s):
a = [[1 2 3] [4 5 6]]

A multidimensional array can be considered as multidimensional matrix. For example

```
a := [3][4]int{
  {0, 1, 2, 3} ,  // initialization of row indexed by 0
  {4, 5, 6, 7} ,  // initialization of row indexed by 1
  {8, 9, 10, 11}  // initialization of row indexed by 2
}
```

Example-7.10: In array declarations, dimension information can be omitted.

```
package main                                    Code
import ("fmt")                                   7.10

func main() {

    var a1 = [...][] int {{}, {}}
    var a2 = [...][] int {{1, 2, 3}, {4}}
    var a3 = [...][3] int {{1, 2, 3}, {4}}

    fmt.Println("a1 = ", a1)
    fmt.Println("a2 = ", a2)
    fmt.Println("a3 = ", a3)
}
```

Output(s):

a1 = [[] []]

a2 = [[1 2 3] [4]]

a3 = [[1 2 3] [4 0 0]]

7.7 Copying Arrays

Arrays can be copied using the assignment operator =.

Example-7.11: In this example, we illustrate array copying.

```
package main                           Code
import ("fmt")                          7.11

func main() {

    var a1 = [4] int {1, 2, 3, 4}
    var a2 = [4] int {}

    a2 = a1

    fmt.Println("a1 = ", a1)
    fmt.Println("a2 = ", a2)

}
```

Output(s):

a1 = [1 2 3 4]

a2 = [1 2 3 4]

Example-7.12: In this example, we illustrate array copying.

```go
package main                            Code
import ("fmt")                          7.12

func main() {

  a1 := [4] int {1, 2, 3, 4}
  a2 := a1

  fmt.Println("a1 = ", a1)
  fmt.Println("a2 = ", a2)
}
```

Output(s):

a1 = [1 2 3 4]

a2 = [1 2 3 4]

Arrays are stored in the memory. The head of the address of the memory block where an array is stored can be obtained as &a where a is the array variable name.

Example-7.13: In this example, we get the array address and print it.

```go
package main                            Code
import ("fmt")                          7.13

func main() {

  var a = [4] int {1, 2, 3, 4}

  fmt.Printf("Array address is: %p", &a)
}
```

Output(s):

Array address is: 0xc0000140a0

7.8 Passing Arrays to Functions

The argument of a function must contain size information as in

```go
        returnType functionName(arrayName [10] int) {

            // statements
        }
```

The argument of the function **cannot** be used without explicit size information as in

```
returnType functionName(arrayName[...] int) {

    // statements
}
```

The function can be called as

```
functionName(a)
```

where a is the array name.

Example-7.14: In this example, we show how to pass an array to a function.

```package main``` ```import "fmt"```	**Code** **7.14**

```go
package main
import "fmt"

func printArray(a [5] int) {

  fmt.Print(a)

}

func main() {

  a := [5] int {1, 2, 3, 4, 5}

  printArray(a)
}
```

Output(s):
[1 2 3 4 5]

Example-7.15: For-loop can be used to display array elements.

```package main```	**Code** **7.15**

```go
package main

import "fmt"

func printArray(a [5] int) {

  for indx :=0; indx < len(a); indx++ {
    fmt.Print(a[indx], " ")
  }
}
func main() {

  a := [5] int {1, 2, 3, 4, 5}

  printArray(a)
}
```

132

Output(s):
1 2 3 4 5

Example-7.16: Code-7.14 cann be written as Code-7.16.

```
package main                                Code
                                            7.16
import "fmt"

func printArray(a [5] int) { // ok

   fmt.Print(a)

}

func main() {

   a := [...] int {1, 2, 3, 4, 5}   // ok

   printArray(a)
}
```

Output(s):
[1 2 3 4 5]

Example-7.17: Code-7.14 cannot be written as Code-7.17.

```
package main                                Code
                                            7.17
import "fmt"

func printArray(a [...] int) { // error
   fmt.Print(a)

}

func main() {

   a := [5] int {1, 2, 3, 4, 5} // ok

   printArray(a)
}
```

Output(s):

Compilation failed due to following error(s)..

Problems

1) Declare an integer array of length 5, and initialize its elements. Print the array elements using a for-loop.

2) What is the output of Code-7.18?

```
package main                                    Code
import "fmt"                                     7.18

func main() {

  a := [5] int {1, 2, 3, 4, 5}

  fmt.Println("Array elements are:")

  for i := 0; i <= 4; i++ {

    fmt.Printf("a[%v] = %v \n",i ,a[i])
  }

}
```

3) Create an array without specifying its size and initialize its elements. After that, print the array elements on the screen.

4) How can you find the length of an array?

5) Print the array elements in Code-7.19 using range keyword.

```
package main                                    Code
import "fmt"                                     7.19

func main() {

  a:= [...] int {1, 2, 3, 4, 5, 6, 7, 8}

  // print the array elemements using range keyword
}
```

6) Initialize the elements of two dimensional array in Code-7.20.

```
package main                                Code
import ("fmt")                              7.20

func main() {

  var a [2][3] int

  // initilize the array elements here

  fmt.Println("a = ", a)
}
```

7) Fill the commas in Code-7.21 such that the function prints the array elements correctly.

```
package main                          Code
                                      7.21
import "fmt"

func printArray(,,,) {

  ///

}

func main() {

  a := [...] int {1, 2, 3, 4, 5}

  printArray(a)
}
```

Chapter-8

Slices in Go

Abstract: In this chapter, we explain slices in Go programming. Slices are similar to arrays with some differences. After their declaration, arrays cannot be resized, whereas slices can be resized. Arrays are value-types, on the other hand, slices are reference-types. Besides, slices have length and capacity parameters, whereas for the arrays only length is defined.

8.1 Slices

For slices, length is the number of elements the slice owns, and capacity is the number of locations reserved for slice. For instance, if length is 8 and capacity is 10, then 10-8 = 2 more locations are reserved for the slice but they are not used yet.

Slices can be declared using the format

```
var sliceName [] dataType {val1, val2, ...}

sliceName := []dataType {val1, val2, ...}
```

or they can be created from an array as

```
sliceName := myArray[a:b]
```

where myArray is an array, and array elements with indexes **a** up to **b-1** are extracted and a slice is formed.
If a is missing, then it is taken as 0, and if b is missing then it is taken as length of array. That is

```
sliceName := myArray[:b]
```
equals to
```
sliceName := myArray[0:b]
```

In a similar manner,
```
sliceName := myArray[a:]
```
equals to
```
sliceName := myArray[a:length of array]
```

136

A slice with N elements can be formed using the make() function as

$$\text{sliceName := make([]dataType, N, M)}$$

where M is the capacity parameter, and if it is not defined, then M equals N.

Note that
$$\text{sliceName := []dataType \{val1, val2, ...\}}$$

is a slice declaration whereas

$$\text{arrName := [...]dataType \{val1, val2, ...\}}$$

is an array declaration.

8.1.1 Zero Valued Slices

The zero valued slices are nil slices. Their length and capacity are zero.

Example-8.1: In this example, we create a nil slice

```
package main                                                    Code
import "fmt"                                                     8.1

func main() {

  slc := []int{}

  fmt.Println("Slice is ", slc)

  fmt.Println("Length and capacity values are", len(slc), cap(slc))
}
```

Output(s):
Slice is []
Length and capacity values are 0 0

Example-8.2: In this example, we create a slice and display it, and its length and capacity.

```
package main                                          Code
import ("fmt")                                         8.2

func main() {

  mySlice := [] int {1, 2, 3}
  fmt.Println(mySlice)
  fmt.Println("Slice length is:", len(mySlice))
  fmt.Println("Slice capacity is:", cap(mySlice))
}
```

Output(s):
[1 2 3]
Slice length is: 3
Slice capacity is: 3

Example-8.3: In this example, we create a slice from an array.

```
package main                                                    Code
import ("fmt")                                                  8.3

func main() {

  arr := [7] int {1, 2, 3, 4, 5, 6, 7}
  slc := arr[3:6]

  fmt.Printf("Array = %v\n", arr)

  fmt.Printf("Slice = %v\n", slc)

  fmt.Printf("arr[3:6] = [arr[3] arr[4] arr[5]]-->[%v %v %v]\n",
             arr[3], arr[4], arr[5])

  fmt.Printf("length = %d\n", len(slc))

  fmt.Printf("capacity = %d\n", cap(slc))
}
```

Output(s):
Array = [1 2 3 4 5 6 7]
Slice = [4 5 6]
arr[3:6] = [arr[3] arr[4] arr[5]]-->[4 5 6]
length = 3
capacity = 4

8.1.2 Length and Capacity Explanations

Assume that we have an array and we create a slice from this array as in Code-8.4.

```
package main                                                  Code
import ("fmt")                                                8.4

func main() {

  arr := [10] int {1, 2, 3, 4, 5, 6, 7, 8, 9, 10}

  slc := arr [3:7]
```

```
                                                      Code
                                                      8.4
fmt.Printf("Array = %v\n", arr)
fmt.Printf("Array capacity = %d\n", cap(arr))
fmt.Printf("Array length = %d\n\n", len(arr))

fmt.Printf("Slice = %v\n", slc)
fmt.Printf("Slice capacity = %d\n", cap(slc))
fmt.Printf("Slice length = %d\n\n", len(slc))
}
```

The outputs of the program are

Array = [1 2 3 4 5 6 7 8 9 10]
Array capacity = 10
Array length = 10

Slice = [4 5 6 7]
Slice capacity = 7
Slice length = 4

The length and capacity values obtained from Code-8.4 are explained in Figure-8.1

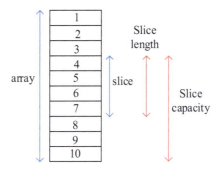

Figure-8.1 Length and capacity explanations for Code-8.4.

Example-8.4: Slice capacity can be equal to array capacity.

```
package main                                          Code
import ("fmt")                                        8.5

func main() {

  arr := [10] int {1, 2, 3, 4, 5, 6, 7, 8, 9, 10}

  slc := arr [:5]
```

```
    fmt.Printf("Array = %v\n", arr)
    fmt.Printf("Array capacity = %d\n", cap(arr))
    fmt.Printf("Array length = %d\n\n", len(arr))

    fmt.Printf("Slice = %v\n", slc)
    fmt.Printf("Slice capacity = %d\n", cap(slc))
    fmt.Printf("Slice length = %d\n\n", len(slc))
}
```

Output(s):
Array = [1 2 3 4 5 6 7 8 9 10]
Array capacity = 10
Array length = 10

Slice = [1 2 3 4 5]
Slice capacity = 10
Slice length = 5

Figure-8.1 Length and capacity explanations for Code-8.5.

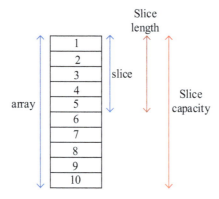

Figure-8.1 Length and capacity explanations for Code-8.5.

Example-8.5: In this example, we show how to create a slice from another slice.

```
package main                                          Code
import ("fmt")                                         8.6

func main() {

  slc := [] int {1, 2, 3, 4, 5, 6, 7, 8, 9, 10}

  slc1 := slc [4:]
  slc2 := slc1 [3:]
```

```
    fmt.Printf("Slice = %v\n", slc)
    fmt.Printf("Slice capacity = %d\n", cap(slc))
    fmt.Printf("Slice length = %d\n\n", len(slc))

    fmt.Printf("Slice1 = %v\n", slc1)
    fmt.Printf("Slice1 capacity = %d\n", cap(slc1))
    fmt.Printf("Slice1 length = %d\n\n", len(slc1))

    fmt.Printf("Slice2 = %v\n", slc2)
    fmt.Printf("Slice2 capacity = %d\n", cap(slc2))
    fmt.Printf("Slice2 length = %d\n", len(slc2))
}
```

Output(s):
Slice = [1 2 3 4 5 6 7 8 9 10]
Slice capacity = 10
Slice length = 10

Slice1 = [5 6 7 8 9 10]
Slice1 capacity = 6
Slice1 length = 6

Slice2 = [8 9 10]
Slice2 capacity = 3
Slice2 length = 3

Example-8.6: Another example for obtaining a slice from another slice.

```
package main                                          Code
import ("fmt")                                         8.7

func main() {

  slc := [] int {1, 2, 3, 4, 5, 6, 7, 8, 9, 10}

  slc1 := slc [4:7]

  fmt.Printf("Slice1 = %v\n", slc1)
  fmt.Printf("Slice1 capacity = %d\n", cap(slc1))
  fmt.Printf("Slice1 length = %d\n\n", len(slc1))
}
```

Output(s):
Slice1 = [5 6 7]
Slice1 capacity = 6
Slice1 length = 3

Example-8.7: In this example, we show how to create a slice with make() function.

```go
package main                                              Code
import ("fmt")                                            8.8

func main() {

  slc := make([]int, 3, 7)

  fmt.Printf("Slice = %v\n", slc)

  slc[0] = 1; slc[1] = 2; slc[2] = 3;

  fmt.Printf("Slice = %v\n", slc)

  fmt.Printf("Slice length = %d\n", len(slc))

  fmt.Printf("Slice capacity = %d\n", cap(slc))
}
```

Output(s):
Slice = [0 0 0]
Slice = [1 2 3]
Slice length = 3
Slice capacity = 7

Example-8.8: In this example, we create a slice with make() function without providing capacity value.

```go
package main                                              Code
import ("fmt")                                            8.9

func main() {

  slc := make([]int, 3)

  slc[0] = 1; slc[1] = 2; slc[2] = 3;

  fmt.Printf("Slice = %v\n", slc)

  fmt.Printf("Slice length = %d\n", len(slc))

  fmt.Printf("Slice capacity = %d\n", cap(slc))
}
```

Output(s):
Slice = [1 2 3]
Slice length = 3
Slice capacity = 3

8.1.3 Appending Slices

Elements can be appended to the end of a slice using the append()function. The append function is used as

$$\text{sliceName = append(sliceName, elm1, elm2, ...)}$$

where elm1, elm2, ... are the elements to be appended to the end of the slice.

Example-8.9: In this example, the use of the append() function is illustrated.

```
package main                                          Code
import "fmt"                                          8.10

func main() {

  slc := [] int {1, 2, 3}
  fmt.Printf("Slice = %v \n", slc)
  fmt.Printf("Slice length = %d\n", len(slc))
  fmt.Printf("Slice capacity = %d\n\n", cap(slc))

  slc = append(slc, 4)
  fmt.Printf("Slice is = %v \n", slc)
  fmt.Printf("Slice length = %d\n", len(slc))
  fmt.Printf("Slice capacity = %d\n\n", cap(slc))

  slc = append(slc, 5, 6, 7, 8)
  fmt.Printf("Slice is = %v \n", slc)
  fmt.Printf("Slice length = %d\n", len(slc))
  fmt.Printf("Slice capacity = %d\n", cap(slc))
}
```

If a new slice is formed using append() function, compiler decides on the capacity of new slice.

Output(s):
Slice = [1 2 3]
Slice length = 3
Slice capacity = 3

Slice is = [1 2 3 4]
Slice length = 4
Slice capacity = 6

Slice is = [1 2 3 4 5 6 7 8]
Slice length = 8
Slice capacity = 12

8.1.4 Concatenating the Slices

Slices can be concatenated using the append function as

$$slc3 := append(slc1, slc2...)$$

where slc1, slc2, slc3 are slices.

Example-8.10: In this example, we concatenate two slices.

```
package main                                              Code
import "fmt"                                              8.11

func main() {

  slc1 := [] int {1, 2}
  slc2 := [] int {3, 4, 5}

  slc3 := append(slc1, slc2...)

  fmt.Println("Slice1 =", slc1)
  fmt.Println("Slice2 =", slc2)
  fmt.Println("Slice3 =", slc3)
}
```

Output(s):
Slice1 = [1 2]
Slice2 = [3 4 5]
Slice3 = [1 2 3 4 5]

Note that only two slices can be used in append function for concatenation. That is, the use of append function in

$$slc4 := append(slc1, slc2, slc3...)$$

is invalid, and error arises in such a use.

8.1.5 Removing Elements from a Slice

Let slc be a slice, then slc[:index] indicates the sub-slice obtained from slc with indexes starting from 0 going up to index-1. Append() function can be used to omit some of the elements of a slice.

Example-8.11: In this example, we illustrate how to use append function to eliminate some of the elements of a slice.

```
package main                                      Code
import "fmt"                                       8.12

func main() {

  slc := [] int {1, 2, 3, 4, 5, 6, 7, 8, 9}

  fmt.Println("Slice =", slc)

  slc = append(slc[:4], slc[6:]...)

  fmt.Println("Slice =", slc)

}
```

Output(s):
Slice = [1 2 3 4 5 6 7 8 9]
Slice = [1 2 3 4 7 8 9]

Problems

1) What is the output of Code-8.13?

```
package main                                          Code
import "fmt"                                           8.13

func main() {

  a := [10] int {3, 7, 8, 99, 5, 34, 21, 0, 12, 45}

  b := a[3:7]

  fmt.Println("Slice b =", b)
}
```

2) How can you find the length of a slice?

3) What is the output of Code-8.14?

```
package main                                          Code
import "fmt"                                           8.14

func main() {

  s := [] string {"I like", "Go",
"programming", "a lot."}

  s1 := s[0 : 4]
  s2 := s[1 : ]
  s3 := s[2 : ]
  s4 := s[ : 4]
  s5 := s[ : 3]
  s6 := s[1 : 3]
  s7 := s[ : ]

  fmt.Println("Slice-1:", s1)
  fmt.Println("Slice-2:", s2)
  fmt.Println("Slice-3:", s3)
  fmt.Println("Slice-4:", s4)
  fmt.Println("Slice-5:", s5)
  fmt.Println("Slice-6:", s6)
  fmt.Println("Slice-7:", s7)
}
```

4) What is the output of Code-8.15?

```
package main                                          Code
import "fmt"                                          8.15

func main() {

  a := [10] int {1, 2, 3, 4, 5, 6, 7, 8, 9, 10}

  s1 := a[2 : 9]
  s2 := s1[3 : 6]

  fmt.Println("s1 =", s1)
  fmt.Println("s2 =", s2)
}
```

5) Create a slice and then using the sort.Ints() function sort the elements of the slice and then print the sorted slice to the screen.

6) What is the output of Code-8.16?

```
package main                                          Code
import "fmt"                                          8.16

var a = [] int {5, 8, 3, 23, 16, 17, 45, 89}

func main() {

  for i, v := range a {

    fmt.Printf("i = %v, v = %v \n", i, v)
  }
}
```

Chapter-9

Maps in Go

Abstract: In this chapter, we explain maps in Go programming. Maps contain key-value pair and they are useful to construct data structures. We explain how to create maps and manipulate maps elements using their keys. Map does not allow duplicate keys and this property is very useful to construct databases. Values of a map can be accessed using keys.

9.1 Maps

Maps can be created using the keyword **var** as

```
var a = map [keyDataType] valueDataType {key1:val1, key2:val2,...}
```

or using the symbol := as

```
a := map [keyDataType] valueDataType {key1:val1, key2:val2,...}
```

Once a map is declared, the values of the map can be accessed using keys as

```
        a[key1]       a[key2]       a[key2]
```

which corresponds to the values

```
        val1      val2      val3
```

The keys of a map **must be distinct**.

9.1.1 Key Data Type

The map key data type should support == operator. The key data type can be one of the numeric, Boolean, string, pointer, channel, interfaces, structs, and array.

The key data type cannot be slice, map or function.

The map values are accessed using

$$a[key]$$

and map values can be changed using

$$m[key] = new\_value$$

If the key does not exist on the map, then the Go compiler returns null.

9.1.2 How to Check Whether a Key Exists or Not?

Assume that 'a' is a map, to check whether a key exist or not we use

$$v, ok := a[key]$$

where if ok is true, then the key exists and the corresponding value is assigned to v, otherwise ok is false and v is "".

Example-9.1: In this example, we create a map and display it.

```
package main                                                    Code
import "fmt"                                                     9.1

func main() {

  var a = map [int] string {6: "Apple", 12: "Orange", 45: "Banana"}

  fmt.Println(a)
}
```

Output(s):
map[6:Apple 12:Orange 45:Banana]

Example-9.2: In this example, we create a map and display its values using its keys

```
package main                                                    Code
import "fmt"                                                     9.2

func main() {

  var a = map [int] string {6: "Apple", 12: "Orange", 45: "Banana"}

  fmt.Println(a[6])
  fmt.Println(a[12])
  fmt.Println(a[45])
}
```

Output(s):

Apple
Orange
Banana

Example-9.3: Keys of a map can be strings.

```
package main                                               Code
import "fmt"                                               9.3

func main() {

  a := map [string] string {"A": "Ford", "B": "BMW", "C": "Mercedes"}

  fmt.Println(a)
}
```

Output(s):
map[A:Ford B:BMW C:Mercedes]

Example-9.4: In this example, we use string keys to print the values.

```
package main                                               Code
import "fmt"                                               9.4

func main() {

  a := map [string] string {"A": "Ford", "B": "BMW", "C": "Audi"}

  fmt.Println(a["A"])
  fmt.Println(a["B"])
  fmt.Println(a["C"])
}
```

Output(s):
Ford
BMW
Mercedes

9.1.3 Map Creation Using make() Function

Maps can be created using the make() function either as

```
var a = make(map[keyDataType] valueDataType)
```
or as
```
a := make(map[keyDataType] valueDataType)
```

Example-9.5: In this example, we create a map using make() function, and assign values using keys. Key data type can be int.

```
package main                                          Code
import ("fmt")                                        9.5

func main() {

  var a = make(map [int] string) //  empty map

  a[1] = "Michael"
  a[2] = "Ilhan"
  a[3] = "Vera"

  fmt.Printf("a --> %v \n", a)
}
```

Output(s):
a --> map[1:Michael 2:Ilhan 3:Vera]

Example-9.6: Key data type can be string.

```
package main                                          Code
import ("fmt")                                        9.6

func main() {

  var a = make(map [string] string) //  empty map

  a["A"] = "Michael"
  a["B"] = "Ilhan"
  a["C"] = "Vera"

  fmt.Printf("a --> %v \n", a)
}
```

Output(s):
a --> map[A:Michael B:Ilhan C:Vera]

9.1.4 Nil Map

A nil map can be created using the make() function as

```
var a map [keyDataType] valueDataType
```

Example-9.7: In this example, we show how to create a nil map.

```
package main                                                    Code
import ("fmt")                                                  9.7

func main() {

  var a = make(map [int] string) // not a nil map

  var b  map [int] string // nil map

  fmt.Println(a == nil)
  fmt.Println(b == nil)
}
```

Output(s):
false
true

Example-9.8: In this example, we check the existence of a key.

```
package main                                                    Code
import "fmt"                                                    9.8

func main() {

  var a = map [string] string {"A": "Yagmur", "B": "Ilhan", "C": "Vera"}
  v, ok := a["B"]

  fmt.Printf("v = %v, ok = %v", v, ok)
}
```

Output(s):
v = Ilhan, ok = true

Example-9.9: This is another example for key checking.

```
package main                                                    Code
import "fmt"                                                    9.9

func main() {

  var a = map [int] string {1: "Yagmur", 2: "Ilhan", 3: "Vera"}

  v, ok := a[5]

  if(v == ""){
    fmt.Println("The key does not exist")
    fmt.Printf("v = %v, ok = %v", v, ok)
  }
}
```

Output(s):
The key does not exist
v = , ok = false

9.1.5 Removing an Element from a Map

The map elements can be removed using the delete() function. The delete() function is used as

```
delete(mapVariableName, key)
```

Example-9.10: In this example, we illustrate the use of the delete() function for a map.

```
package main                                              Code
import "fmt"                                              9.10

func main() {

  var students = map [int] string {2: "Vera", 5: "Ilhan",
                                    8: "Yagmur"}

  fmt.Println(students)
  delete(students, 5)
  fmt.Println(students)
}
```

Output(s):
map[2:Vera 5:Ilhan 8:Yagmur]
map[2:Vera 8:Yagmur]

9.1.6 Map Variables

Map variables are references to some hash tables. If one map variable is equated to another one, then the changes made on the content of one variable are directly seen on the other variable.

Example-9.11: In this example, we show that changes on one variable can affect another one.

```
package main                                              Code
import "fmt"                                              9.11

func main() {

  var a = map [int] string {6: "Apple", 12: "Orange", 45: "Banana"}
  b := a

  fmt.Println("a --> ", a)
  b[12] = "Grape"
  fmt.Println("a --> ", a)
}
```

Output(s):

a --> map[6:Apple 12:Orange 45:Banana]

a --> map[6:Apple 12:Grape 45:Banana]

9.1.7 Accessing the Elements of a Map Using For-Loop

The elements of a map can be read using a for-loop and range keyword. The syntax is given as

```
for key, value := range mapName {

    // statements
}
```

Example-9.13:

```
package main                                              Code
import "fmt"                                               9.12

func main() {

  var grades = map [string] int { "AA": 90, "BB": 80,
                                  "CC": 70, "DD": 60 }

  for key, value := range grades {

    fmt.Println("Key:", key, "=>", "Value:", value)
  }
}
```

Output(s):

Key: AA => Value: 90

Key: BB => Value: 80

Key: CC => Value: 70

Key: DD => Value: 60

Problems

1) What is the output of Code-9.13?

```
package main                                                      Code
import "fmt"                                                      9.13

func main() {

  studentNumbers := make( map [string] int)

  studentNumbers["Jack"]  = 2345
  studentNumbers["Vera"]  = 7898
  studentNumbers["Ilhan"] = 5647
  studentNumbers["Klaus"] = 7688
  studentNumbers["Arif"]  = 1254

  fmt.Println("Jack:",  studentNumbers["Jack"])
  fmt.Println("Vera:",  studentNumbers["Vera"])
  fmt.Println("Ilhan:", studentNumbers["Ilhan"])
  fmt.Println("Klaus:", studentNumbers["Klaus"])
  fmt.Println("Arif:",  studentNumbers["Arif"])
}
```

2) Delete the item with key Ilhan from the map of the previous problem.

3) How can you find the number of elements in a map?

4) Fill the dots in Code-9.14 to display the map keys and values.

```
package main                                                      Code
import "fmt"                                                      9.14

func main() {

  studentNumbers := make( map [string] int)

  studentNumbers["Jack"]  = 2345
  studentNumbers["Vera"]  = 7898
  studentNumbers["Ilhan"] = 5647
  studentNumbers["Klaus"] = 7688
  studentNumbers["Arif"]  = 1254

  for k, v := range ... {
    ...
  }
}
```

5) Create a copy of the map in Code-9.13.

6) Add 3 new elements to the map of Code-9.15.

```
package main                                    Code
import "fmt"                                     9.15

func main() {

  grades := map [int] string {1: "AA", 2: "AB"}

  fmt.Println("Grades: ", grades)

  ... // add element with key 3

  ... // add element with key 4

  ... // add element with key 12

  fmt.Println("Grades: ", grades)
}
```

7) In Code-9.16, myMap is a map variable. What is the meaning of underscore in Code-9.16?

```
for _, v := range myMap {        Code
                                  9.16
      //
}
```

Chapter-10

Pointers in Go

Abstract: In this chapter, we explain pointers in Go programming. Pointers are one of the most important topics of every programming language. It is especially important for hardware engineers. Go has automatic garbage collector, this means that unused memory locations are freed automatically, and this makes go an efficient programming language. In Go, use of pointers for structure data types is easier compared to other programming languages.

10.1 Introduction

A pointer is a variable which keeps the address of another variable it points to. The data type of the pointer should be the same as the data type of the variable the pointer points to.

The syntax for pointer variable declaration is as

var pointerVariableName* pointedDataType

where pointed data type can be any Go data type, and pointer variable name can be chosen as any variable name.

For instance, we can declare an integer pointer as

var ptr* int

10.2 Address Operator

Pointers are initialized to the address of the variables, and address of the variables are obtained using the address operator **&**. If a is a variable, then the address of a is obtained as &a.

The contend of an address is obtained using the dereferencing operator *, i.e.,

*address = content of the address;

For instance, if

$$\textbf{var} \ a \ int = 25$$

then

$$*(\&a) \ equals \ 25$$

A pointer can also be declared using address operator without using * in the declaration as

$$\textbf{var} \ ptr = \&a$$

where the type of the pointer is determined by the compiler considering the type of the pointed variable.

Example-10.1: In this example, we show how to use address and dereferencing operators.

```
package main                                    Code
import "fmt"                                     10.1

func main() {

  var a int   = 25;
  var ptr* int = &a

  fmt.Printf("Address of a: %v \n", ptr)
  fmt.Printf("Address of a: %v \n", &a)

  fmt.Printf("Value of a: %d \n", *ptr);
  fmt.Printf("Value of a: %d", *(&a));
}
```

Output(s):
Address of a: 0xc000016058
Address of a: 0xc000016058
Value of a: 25
Value of a: 25

Pointer variables hold 8 bytes, i.e., 64 bits, in memory.

Example-10.2: In this example, we show that the size of an integer pointer is 8 bytes.

```
package main                                           Code
import "fmt"                                            10.2
import "unsafe"

func main() {

  var a int   = 25;
  var ptr* int = &a
  fmt.Printf("Size of pointer: %v bytes \n",unsafe.Sizeof(ptr))
}
```

Output(s): Size of pointer: 8 bytes
In Go an uninitialized pointer will always have a nil value.

Example-10.3: Uninitialized pointers have default nil value.

```
package main                                    Code
import "fmt"                                     10.3

func main() {

  var ptr* int

  fmt.Printf("ptr: %d\n", ptr)
  fmt.Printf("ptr: %p\n", ptr)
  fmt.Printf("ptr: %v", ptr)
}
```

Output(s):
ptr: 0
ptr: 0x0
ptr: <nil>

If the pointer type is not indicated, its type can also be determined by the compiler like a normal variable.

Example-10.4: In this example, automatic detection of pointer type is illustrated.

```
package main                                    Code
import "fmt"                                     10.4

func main() {

  var a = 25
  var ptr = &a

  fmt.Printf("Address of a: %v \n", ptr)

  fmt.Printf("Type of ptr: %T \n", ptr)

  fmt.Printf("Value of a: %d ", *ptr)
}
```

Output(s):
Address of a: 0xc000016058
Type of ptr: *int
Value of a: 25

We can use the symbol := to define the pointers in Go.

Example-10.5: In this example, we use the assignment symbol := to define a pointer.

```
package main                                    Code
import "fmt"                                     10.5

func main() {

  a := 45.7
  ptr := &a

  fmt.Printf("Address of a: %v \n", ptr)

  fmt.Printf("Type of ptr: %T \n", ptr)

  fmt.Printf("Value of a: %v \n", *ptr)
}
```

Output(s):
Address of a: 0xc000016058
Type of ptr: *float64
Value of a: 45.7

Example-10.6: Pointers can be used for any data type.

```
package main                                    Code
import "fmt"                                     10.6

func main() {

  a := "Hello World"
  ptr := &a

  fmt.Printf("a: %v \n", a)
  fmt.Printf("&a: %v \n\n", &a)

  fmt.Printf("ptr: %v \n", ptr)
  fmt.Printf("*ptr: %v \n", *ptr)
}
```

Output(s):
a: Hello World
&a: 0xc00007c1c0

ptr: 0xc00007c1c0
*ptr: Hello World

Pointers hold the address of variables. If the content of the address is changed by dereferencing operator, *, the value of the variable changes as well.

Example-10.7: In this example, we show how to change the value of a variable using dereferencing operator *.

```
package main                      Code
import "fmt"                      10.7

func main() {

    a := 38
    ptr := &a

    fmt.Printf("a: %v \n", a)

    *ptr = 45

    fmt.Printf("a: %v \n", a)
}
```

Output(s):
a: 38
a: 45

Example-10.8: Another example for dereferencing operator *.

```
package main                      Code
import "fmt"                      10.8

func main() {

    a := "Hello World"
    ptr := &a

    fmt.Printf("a: %v \n", a)

    *ptr = "How are You?"

    fmt.Printf("a: %v \n", a)
}
```

Output(s):
a: Hello World
a: How are You?

10.3 Pointer Arithmetic in Go

Unlike C, Go has no pointer arithmetic. That is, if ptr is a pointer variable, e.g., we do not have ptr++ operation.

10.4 Pointer Pointing Another Pointer

A pointer points to a variable, and a pointer is a variable, which means a pointer can point to another pointer.

Example-10.9: In this example, pointer pointing to another pointer is illustrated.

```
package main                                      Code
import "fmt"                                       10.9

func main() {

  var a int32 = 0x12345678

  ptr1 := &a
  ptr2 := &ptr1

  fmt.Printf("ptr1: %v \n", ptr1)
  fmt.Printf("ptr2: %v \n\n", ptr2)

  fmt.Printf("*ptr1: %#X \n", *ptr1)
  fmt.Printf("*ptr2: %#x \n", *ptr2)
}
```

Output(s):
ptr1: 0xc000016058
ptr2: 0xc00000e028

*ptr1: 0X12345678
*ptr2: 0xc000016058

In Figure-10.1, the relations between addresses and values are illustrated. In Figure-10.1, little-endian convention is used.

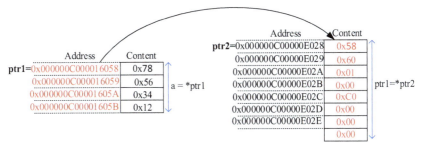

Figure-10.1 Visual explanation of Example-10.9.

Example-10.10: A pointer can point to another pointer.

```
package main                                    Code
import "fmt"                                     10.10

func main() {

  var a int = 0x12345678

  var ptr1* int = &a
  var ptr2** int = &ptr1
  var ptr3*** int = &ptr2
  var ptr4**** int = &ptr3

  fmt.Printf("ptr1: %v \n", ptr1)
  fmt.Printf("ptr2: %v \n", ptr2)
  fmt.Printf("ptr3: %v \n", ptr3)
  fmt.Printf("ptr4: %v \n", ptr4)
}
```

Output(s):
ptr1: 0xc000098020
ptr2: 0xc00009a018
ptr3: 0xc00009a020
ptr4: 0xc00009a028

Example-10.11: Another example illustrating the pointers pointing to other pointers.

```
package main                                    Code
import "fmt"                                     10.11

func main() {

  var a int = 0x12345678
```

163

```go
    var ptr1* int = &a
    var ptr2** int = &ptr1
    var ptr3*** int = &ptr2
    var ptr4**** int = &ptr3

    fmt.Printf("ptr1: %v \n", ptr1)
    fmt.Printf("*ptr2: %v \n\n", *ptr2)
    fmt.Printf("ptr2: %v \n", ptr2)
    fmt.Printf("*ptr3: %v \n\n", *ptr3)
    fmt.Printf("ptr3: %v \n", ptr3)
    fmt.Printf("*ptr4: %v \n\n", *ptr4)
    fmt.Printf("ptr4: %v \n", ptr4)
}
```

Output(s):
ptr1: 0xc000016058
*ptr2: 0xc000016058

ptr2: 0xc00000e028
*ptr3: 0xc00000e028

ptr3: 0xc00000e030
*ptr4: 0xc00000e030

ptr4: 0xc00000e038

Example-10.12: Addresses can be tracked in a chained manner to arrive in the final value.

```go
package main                                    Code
import "fmt"                                     10.12

func main() {

  var a int = 0x12345678

  var ptr1* int = &a
  var ptr2** int = &ptr1
  var ptr3*** int = &ptr2
  var ptr4**** int = &ptr3

  fmt.Printf("*ptr1: %#x \n", *ptr1)
  fmt.Printf("**ptr2: %#x \n", **ptr2)
  fmt.Printf("***ptr3: %#x \n", ***ptr3)
  fmt.Printf("****ptr4: %#x \n", ****ptr4)
}
```

Output(s):
*ptr1: 0x12345678
**ptr2: 0x12345678
***ptr3: 0x12345678
****ptr4: 0x12345678

10.5 Pointers in Function Arguments

Pointers are variables used to store addresses of other variables, and like any variable pointers can also be passed to function arguments.

Example-10.13: In this example, we use a function whose argument contains a pointer.

```
package main                                        Code
import "fmt"                                         10.13

func main() {

  var a int = 56

  fmt.Printf("Before function call, a =  %v \n", a)
  fmt.Printf("Before function call, &a =  %v \n\n", &a)

  myFunc(&a)

  fmt.Printf("After function call, a =  %v \n", a)
  fmt.Printf("After function call, &a =  %v \n\n", &a)
}

func myFunc(b* int) {

  fmt.Printf("Inside function, b =  %v \n", b)

  *b = 87

  fmt.Printf("Inside function, *b =  %v \n\n", *b)
}
```

Output(s):
Before function call, a = 56
Before function call, &a = 0xc000090020

Inside function, b = 0xc000090020
Inside function, *b = 87

After function call, a = 87
After function call, &a = 0xc000090020

10.6 Functions Returning Pointers

In C programming, returning the address of a local variable of a function creates problem, since function variables are stored in the stack, and when the function exits the local variables of the function are removed from the stack.

However, in Go programming things are different. The Go compiler does not use the stack to store the local variables of a function; instead, it uses heap memory to store the local variables of the function. For this reason, returning addresses of local variables of a function does not create a problem; however, this is a serious problem in C programming.

Example-10.14: In this example we use a function which returns a pointer.

```
package main                                      Code
import "fmt"                                       10.14

func myFunc()(p* int) {

  var a int = 89 // local variable is stored at heap memory
                 // not at stack
  p = &a

  return
}

func main() {

  ptr := myFunc();

  fmt.Printf("Pointed address is: %p \n", ptr)

  fmt.Printf("Value at address is: %v \n", *ptr)
}
```

Output(s):
Pointed address is: 0xc000098020
Value at address is: 89

The function in Code-10.14 can be written as in Code-10.15.

```
func myFunc() (*int) {            Code
                                   10.15
  var a int = 89
  p := &a
  return p
}
```

10.7 Function Pointers

The name of a function is nothing but a pointer pointing to the memory block inside function implementation is stored.

Example-10.15:

```
package main                                        Code
import "fmt"                                         10.16
import "unsafe"

func main() {

  fp := myFunc

  fmt.Printf("fp: %p\n", fp)

  fmt.Printf("Size of fp: %d \n", unsafe.Sizeof(fp))

  fp()
}
```

Output(s):
fp: 0x488e50
Size of fp: 8
Hello World!

10.8 Array of Pointers

Like any other variables, we can declare pointer arrays. A pointer array is declared as

$$\text{var ptr [arrayLength] * dataType}$$

Example-10.16: We use a pointer array in this example.

```
package main                                        Code
import "fmt"                                         10.17

func main() {

  a := [3] int {5, 7, 12}

  var ptr [3] * int

  for  indx := 0; indx < 3; indx++ {

    ptr[indx] = &a[indx]
  }
```

```go
for  indx := 0; indx < 3; indx++ {

    fmt.Printf("ptr[%d] = %p\n", indx, ptr[indx] )
    fmt.Printf("*ptr[%d] = %d\n\n", indx, *ptr[indx] )
  }
}
```

Output(s):
ptr[0] = 0xc00009e000
*ptr[0] = 5

ptr[1] = 0xc00009e008
*ptr[1] = 7

ptr[2] = 0xc00009e010
*ptr[2] = 12

10.9 Pointer to a Struct

A structure variable can be pointed by a pointer using address operator & as in the case of other variables. However, in Go programming, dereferencing operator is not needed to access the fields of a structure. The fields of a structure can be accessed directly using the pointer without employing dereferencing operator.

Example-10.17:

```go
package main                                      Code
import "fmt"                                       10.18

type person struct {

  name string
  age int
}
func main() {

  // p := person {"Ilhan", 38}; ptr = &p
  ptr := &person {"Ilhan", 38}

  fmt.Println("ptr:", ptr)
  fmt.Println("*ptr:", *ptr, "\n")

  fmt.Println("name:", ptr.name)
  fmt.Println("age:", ptr.age, "\n")

  fmt.Println("name:", (*ptr).name)
  fmt.Println("age:", (*ptr).age)
}
```

Output(s):
ptr: &{Ilhan 38}
*ptr: {Ilhan 38}

name: Ilhan
age: 38

name: Ilhan
age: 38

10.10 Creating Pointers by the New Function

The prototype of the **new**() function is as

$$\textbf{func } new(dataType) \ \ *dataType$$

For single variables the new function can be used as

$$new(dataType)$$

For array creation it can be used as

$$new([array\_size]dataType)$$

For instance

$$\textbf{var } p* \ [] \ int = new([]int)$$

The new() function is used to allocate memory for variables of different data types, such as integers, floats, structs, etc, and the function returns a pointer to the allocated regions and allocated regions are initialized by zeros.

Example-10.18: In this example we use new function to allocate space for an **int32** variable.

```
package main                                          Code
import "fmt"                                          10.19

func main() {

  var ptr* int32 = new (int32)

  *ptr = 10

  fmt.Printf("Pointer type is: %T \n", ptr)
  fmt.Printf("Pointed address is: %p \n", ptr)
  fmt.Printf("Value at address is: %v \n", *ptr)
}
```

Output(s):
Pointer type is: *int32
Pointed address is: 0xc000016058
Value at address is: 10

Example-10.19: In this example we use new function to allocate space for an **int** variable.

```
package main                                      Code
import "fmt"                                       10.20

func main() {

  a := new (int)

  *a = 56

  fmt.Printf("Pointer type is: %T \n", a)
  fmt.Printf("Pointed address is: %p \n", a)
  fmt.Printf("Value at address is: %v \n", *a)
}
```

Output(s):
Pointer type is: *int
Pointed address is: 0xc000088010
Value at address is: 56

Example-10.20: In this example we use new function to allocate space for a **string** variable.

```
package main                                      Code
import "fmt"                                       10.21

func main() {

  s := new (string)

  *s = "Hello World!"

  fmt.Printf("Pointer type is: %T \n", s)
  fmt.Printf("Pointed address is: %p \n", s)
  fmt.Printf("Value at address is: %v \n", *s)
}
```

Output(s):
Pointer type is: *string
Pointed address is: 0xc0000101e0
Value at address is: Hello World!

Example-10.21: In this example we use new function to allocate space for a **struct** variable.

```
package main                              Code
import "fmt"                              10.22

type student struct {
  name string
  num  int
}

func main() {

  ptr := new(student)

  ptr.name = "Vera"
  ptr.num = 124567

  fmt.Printf("Pointer type is: %T \n", ptr)
  fmt.Printf("Pointed address is: %p \n", ptr)
  fmt.Printf("Pointed value is: %v \n\n", *ptr)

  fmt.Println("Student name is:", ptr.name)
  fmt.Println("Student number is:", ptr.num)
}
```

Output(s):
Pointer type is: *main.student
Pointed address is: 0xc00000c060
Pointed value is: {Vera 124567}

Student name is: Vera
Student number is: 124567

Example-10.22: In this example we use new function to allocate space for an **int array** variable.

```
package main                              Code
import "fmt"                              10.23

func main() {

  var ptr* [4] int = new([4] int)
  fmt.Printf("*ptr = %v \n", *ptr)

  ptr[0]  = 3; ptr[1]  = 5;
  ptr[2]  = 7; ptr[3]  = 10

  fmt.Printf("Pointer type is: %T \n", ptr)
  fmt.Printf("ptr = %p \n", ptr)
  fmt.Printf("*ptr = %v \n", *ptr)
}
```

171

Output(s):
*ptr = [0 0 0 0]
Pointer type is: *[4]int
ptr = 0xc0000140c0
*ptr = [3 5 7 10]

Example-10.23: In this example we use new function to allocate space for an empty slice.

```
package main                                    Code
import "fmt"                                     10.24

func main() {

  var ptr* [] int = new([] int)

  fmt.Printf("Pointer type is: %T \n", ptr)
  fmt.Printf("ptr = %p \n", ptr)
  fmt.Printf("ptr = %v \n", ptr)
  fmt.Printf("*ptr = %v \n", *ptr)
}
```

Output(s):
Pointer type is: *[]int
ptr = 0xc00000c060
ptr = &[]
*ptr = []

Example-10.24: Even an empty slice pointer can be used to point other slices.

```
package main                                    Code
import "fmt"                                     10.25

func main() {

  var a = [] int {1, 2, 3, 4}
  var ptr* [] int = new([] int)
  ptr = &a

  fmt.Printf("Pointer type is: %T \n", ptr)
  fmt.Printf("ptr = %p \n", ptr)
  fmt.Printf("ptr = %v \n", ptr)
  fmt.Printf("*ptr = %v \n", *ptr)
}
```

Output(s):
Pointer type is: *[]int
ptr = 0xc00000c060
ptr = &[1 2 3 4]
*ptr = [1 2 3 4]

Example-10.25: In this example, we allocate space for an array using new function, and the created pointer points to another array. Memory is wasted in this example.

```
package main                              Code
import "fmt"                              10.26

func main() {

  var a = [4] int {1, 2, 3, 4}

  var ptr* [4] int = new([4] int)

  ptr = &a

  fmt.Printf("Pointer type is: %T \n", ptr)
  fmt.Printf("ptr = %p \n", ptr)
  fmt.Printf("*ptr = %v \n", *ptr)
}
```

Output(s):
Pointer type is: *[4]int
ptr = 0xc00009e000
*ptr = [1 2 3 4]

Example-10.26: We allocate space for an array using new function different than in the previous example, and the created pointer points to another array. Memory is wasted in this example.

```
package main                              Code
import "fmt"                              10.27

func main() {

  var a = [4] int {1, 2, 3, 4}

  ptr := new([4] int)

  ptr = &a

  fmt.Printf("Pointer type is: %T \n", ptr)
  fmt.Printf("ptr = %p \n", ptr)
  fmt.Printf("*ptr = %v \n", *ptr)
}
```

Output(s):
Pointer type is: *[4]int
ptr = 0xc0000140a0
*ptr = [1 2 3 4]

Example-10.27: In this example, we do NOT allocate space for an array using new function, the pointer points to an array. Memory is NOT wasted.

```
package main                                              Code
import "fmt"                                              10.28

func main() {

  var a = [4] int {1, 2, 3, 4}

  var ptr* [4] int

  ptr = &a

  fmt.Printf("Pointer type is: %T \n", ptr)
  fmt.Printf("ptr = %p \n", ptr)
  fmt.Printf("*ptr = %v \n", *ptr)
}
```

Output(s):
Pointer type is: *[4]int
ptr = 0xc00009e000
*ptr = [1 2 3 4]

10.11 Make Function for Memory Allocation

The general form of the make() function is as

```
func make(dataType, optionalArg1, optionalAr2) dataType
```

The make() function returns the value of data type, it does NOT return a pointer.

The syntax of the make function varies depending on the data type it is used for.

For slices, the make function is used as

```
func make([]dataType, length, capacity) [] dataType
```

For maps, the make function is used as

```
func make(map[keyDataType] valueDataType, initCapacity int)
         map[keyDataType] valueDataType
```

For channels, the make function is used as

```
func make(chan dataType, capacity int) chan dataType
```

174

```
make([]int, 10, 100)
```

allocates an array of 100 integers and then creates a slice structure with length 10 and a capacity of 100 pointing at the first 10 elements of the array.

Example-10.28: In this example, we create an int array using make() function.

```
package main                                      Code
import "fmt"                                       10.29

func main() {

  var a [] int = make([] int, 4)

  fmt.Println("Length:", len(a))
  fmt.Println("Capacity:", cap(a))
  fmt.Println("Values:", a)
}
```

Output(s):
Length: 4
Capacity: 4
Values: [0 0 0 0]

Example-10.29: In this example, we create an int32 array using make() function.

```
package main                                      Code
import "fmt"                                       10.30

func main() {

  a := make([] int32, 5, 7)

  fmt.Println("Length:", len(a))
  fmt.Println("Capacity:", cap(a))
  fmt.Println("Values:", a)
}
```

Output(s):
Length: 5
Capacity: 7
Values: [0 0 0 0 0]

Example-10.30: In this example, we create a map using make() function.

```
package main                                    Code
import "fmt"                                     10.31

func main() {

    marks := make(map [string] int)

    marks["Ilhan"] = 67
    marks["Vera"] = 93

    fmt.Println("Marks:", marks)
}
```

Output(s):
Marks: map[Ilhan:67 Vera:93]

Example-10.31: In this example, we create a channel using make() function, and use the channel for data sending/receiving operations.

```
package main                                              Code
import "fmt"                                              10.32
import "time"

func main() {

    channel := make(chan int)

    // transmitting data through the channel using a go routine

    go func() {

        for d := 0; d < 4; d++ {

            channel <- d

            fmt.Println("Transmitted value:", d)

            time.Sleep(time.Second) // create some delay
        }
        close(channel)
    }()

    for r := range channel { // receiving data through the channel

        fmt.Println("Received value:", r)
    }
}
```

Output(s):

Transmitted value: 0
Received value: 0
Transmitted value: 1
Received value: 1
Transmitted value: 2
Received value: 2
Transmitted value: 3
Received value: 3

Problems

1) Find the output of Code-10.33.

```
package main                              Code
import "fmt"                              10.33

func main() {

  var a int = 67
  var ptr* int = &a

  fmt.Printf("a = %v\n", a)
  fmt.Printf("*ptr = %v\n\n", *ptr)

  *ptr = 29

  fmt.Printf("a = %v \n", a)
  fmt.Printf("*ptr = %v", *ptr)
}
```

2) Find the output of Code-10.34.

```
package main                              Code
import "fmt"                              10.34

func main() {

  var a float64 = 78.67
  var ptr* float64 = &a

  fmt.Printf("a = %v\n", a)
  fmt.Printf("*ptr = %v\n\n", *ptr)

  *ptr = 45.89

  fmt.Printf("a = %v \n", a)
  fmt.Printf("*ptr = %v", *ptr)
}
```

3) Find the output of Code-10.35.

```
package main                                          Code
import "fmt"                                          10.35

func main() {

  var a int = 68
  var ptr1* int
  var ptr2** int
  var ptr3*** int

  ptr1 = &a
  ptr2 = &ptr1
  ptr3 = &ptr2

  fmt.Printf("a = %d\n", a)
  fmt.Printf("*ptr1   = %v \n", *ptr1)
  fmt.Printf("**ptr2 = %v \n", **ptr2)
  fmt.Printf("***ptr3 = %v \n", ***ptr3)

  ***ptr3 = 124
  fmt.Printf("a = %d\n", a)
  fmt.Printf("*ptr1   = %v \n", *ptr1)
  fmt.Printf("**ptr2 = %v \n", **ptr2)
  fmt.Printf("***ptr3 = %v \n", ***ptr3)
}
```

4) Run the program in Code-10.36, draw memory locations and show how the outputs are stored in registers.

```
package main                                          Code
import "fmt"                                          10.36

func main() {

  var a int32 = 0x1ABCDEF9

  ptr1 := &a
  ptr2 := &ptr1

  fmt.Printf("ptr1: %v \n", ptr1)
  fmt.Printf("ptr2: %v \n\n", ptr2)

  fmt.Printf("*ptr1: %#X \n", *ptr1)
  fmt.Printf("*ptr2: %#x \n", *ptr2)
}
```

5) Fill in the dots in Code-10.37.

```
package main                                          Code
import "fmt"                                          10.37

type car struct {

  model string
  color string
  production_year int
}

func main() {

  p :=  car {...}; // define a car object here

  // declare a pointer and point to p
  ...

  // and print the struct members using pointer
  ...
}
```

6) Fill in the dots in Code-10.38.

```
package main                                          Code
import "fmt"                                          10.38

func main() {

  var ptr* int32 = ... // use new() to create a pointer

  ... ptr = ... // assign 46 to the pointer value

  fmt.Printf(...) // print Pointer type
  fmt.Printf(...) // print Pointer address
  fmt.Printf(...) // print Pointer value
}
```

7) Fill in the dots in Code-10.39.

```
package main                                          Code
import "fmt"                                          10.39

func main() {

  a := make(...) // allocate an integer array
                 // with length 6 and capacity 10

  ... // initialize the array elements
  ... // print array elements
  ... // print array length
  ... // print array capacity
  ... // print array elements
}
```

Chapter-11

Concurrency in Go

Abstract: In this chapter, we explain concurrency in Go programming. Parallel processing is possible in Go programming using routines. Go routines are easy to use for writing programs for parallel processing. It is also possible to write race free programs in Go, and this is achieved either using mutex function or using atomic function and variables.

11.1 Go Routines

A go-routine is similar to the thread in the Go programming language, but, a go routine is much simpler than a thread and it can be considered as a lightweight execution thread. The go-routine executes concurrently with other program units.

A go function can be converted to a go-routine simply by using the keyword **go** as a prefix to the function. The syntax is as

```
func fuctionName(){

  // statements
}

// use prefix go before the function name

go fuctionName()
```

Example-11.1: Our first go-routine is written in Code-11.1.

```
package main                                    Code
import "fmt"                                     11.1
//import "time"

func myFunc(msg string) {

    fmt.Println(msg)
}
```

```
func main() {

  go myFunc("Hello World")

}
```

When the Code-11.1 is executed, we don't see anything at the output. The reason for this is that the compiler does not wait for go-routine to complete its execution like a normal function. The compiler moves forward to the next line after the go-routine call, and quits the main program before the go-routine completes its execution.

We can use time.Sleep() function to create an artificial delay. The prototype of the function is

func Sleep(d Duration)

where d is the duration of time to sleep. The function is defined in the "time" package.

The function is used as

time.Sleep(d * timeunit)

where

d	is the duration
*	is the multiplication operation
timeunit	can be time.Nanosecond, time.Microsecond, time.Millisecond, time.Second, time.Minute and time.Hour

Let's assume that we want to pause a process for 4 seconds. We can use the Sleep function as

time.Sleep(4 * time.Second)

which can also be written as

time.Sleep(time.Duration(4) * time.Second)

To create a 0.5 second delay we can use the Sleep function as

time.Sleep(500 * time.Millisecond)

Example-11.2: We add 0.5 second delay to the Code-11.1 and obtain Code-11.2.

```go
package main                                          Code
import "fmt"                                          11.2
import "time"

func myFunc(msg string) {

  fmt.Println(msg)
}

func main() {

  go myFunc("Hello World!")

  time.Sleep(500 * time.Millisecond) // 0.5 second delay
}
```

When Code-11.2 is executed, we get the output "Hello World!"

Example-11.3: In this example we use two go-routines, and both routines involve infinite loops.

```go
package main                                          Code
import "fmt"                                          11.3
import "time"

func myFunc1() {

  for {

    fmt.Println("Inside myFunc1")
    time.Sleep(time.Second) // one second delay
  }
}
func myFunc2() {

  for {

    fmt.Println("Inside myFunc2")
    time.Sleep(time.Second) // one second delay
  }
}
func main() {

  go myFunc1()
  go myFunc2()

  for { // infinite loop

    time.Sleep(time.Second) // one second delay
    fmt.Println("Inside Main")
  }
}
```

Output(s):
Inside myFunc1
Inside myFunc2
Inside Main
Inside myFunc2
Inside myFunc1
Inside Main
....

Example-11.4: In this example we use one go function for two go-routines.

```go
package main                                          Code
import "fmt"                                          11.4
import "time"

func myFunc(msg string) {

  for true {

    fmt.Println(msg)
    time.Sleep(time.Second) // one second delay

  }
}

func main() {

  go myFunc("Hello World1")
  go myFunc("Hello World2")

  for true { // infinite loop

    time.Sleep(time.Second) // one second delay
    fmt.Println("Inside Main")
  }

}
```

Output(s):
Hello World1
Hello World2
Inside Main
Hello World2
Hello World1
Inside Main
....

11.2 Wait for all Go-Routines to Finish

Sleep() function solves the problem of early termination, but it is usually used for illustration purposes. In applications, it is not practical to use the Sleep() function. Go provides "sync" package containing WaitGroup library which solves early termination problem.

Example-11.5: In Code-11.5, we use three wait group functions, and we eliminate the use of the sleep function as in Code-11.4.

```
package main                                    Code
import "fmt"                                     11.5
import "sync"

var wg sync.WaitGroup

func main() {

  wg.Add(1) // there is one go-routine

  go myFunc()

  fmt.Println("Inside main function")

  wg.Wait()
}

func myFunc() {

  defer wg.Done()

  fmt.Println("Inside myFunc")
}
```

Output(s):
Inside main function
Inside myFunc

Explanation:

In Code-11.5, we create an instance of sync.WaitGroup. Since, we have only one go-routine, we call wg.Add(1). defer wg.Done() in each go-routine is used, done method is called by each of the go-routines when finished. The function wg.Wait() is used to assure that all go-routines have finished and have called the Done() method.

Example-11.6: In Code-11.5, we use a global variable for sync.WaitGroup. We can use a local variable for sync.WaitGroup as in Code-11.6. However, in this case the arguments of go-routines contain the pointer variable "wg* sync.WaitGroup", and routine is called using &wg as in Code-11.6.

186

```go
package main                                          Code
import "fmt"                                          11.6
import "sync"

func main() {

  var wg sync.WaitGroup // local variable

  wg.Add(1) // there is one go-routine

  go myFunc(&wg)

  fmt.Println("Inside main function")

  wg.Wait()
}

func myFunc(wg* sync.WaitGroup) {

  defer wg.Done()

  fmt.Println("Inside myFunc")
}
```

Output(s):
Inside main function
Inside myFunc

Example-11.7: In this example, we will use two go-routines, and the main program waits until all the routines finished with their tasks. First, we write the main part, and declare the variable wg for sync.WaitGroup as in Code-11.7.

```go
package main                                          Code
import "fmt"                                          11.7
import "sync"
import "time"

func main() {

  var wg sync.WaitGroup


}
```

There will be two go-routines, for this reason we use the wg.Add() function with argument 2 as in Code-11.8.

```
package main                                          Code
import "fmt"                                          11.8
import "sync"
import "time"

func main() {

  var wg sync.WaitGroup

  wg.Add(2) // there are 2 go-routines

}
```

Assume that the names of the functions are myFunc1, and myFunc2, we declare these function as go-routines as in Code-11.9. Besides, in Code-11.9, we use wg.Wait() function so that main program does not terminate until all the routines finish their tasks.

```
package main                                          Code
import "fmt"                                          11.9
import "sync"
import "time"

func main() {

  var wg sync.WaitGroup
  wg.Add(2) // there are 2 go-routines

  go myFunc1(&wg)
  go myFunc2(&wg)

  fmt.Println("Inside main")

  wg.Wait()
}
```

We start writing go-routines as in Code-11.10 where defer wg.Done() functions are placed inside both routines.

```
package main                                          Code
import "fmt"                                          11.10
import "sync"
import "time"

func main() {

  var wg sync.WaitGroup
  wg.Add(2) // there are 2 go-routines
```

```
   go myFunc1(&wg)
   go myFunc2(&wg)

   fmt.Println("Inside main")

   wg.Wait()
}

func myFunc1(wg *sync.WaitGroup) {

   defer wg.Done()
}

func myFunc2(wg *sync.WaitGroup) {

   defer wg.Done()
}
```

Finally, bodies of the functions are written as in Code-11.11, and we get the entire program which contains two go-routines which run in parallel.

```
package main                              Code
import "fmt"                              11.11
import "sync"
import "time"

func main() {

  var wg sync.WaitGroup

  wg.Add(2) // there are 2 go-routines

  go myFunc1(&wg)
  go myFunc2(&wg)

  fmt.Println("Inside main")

  wg.Wait()
}
func myFunc1(wg *sync.WaitGroup) {

  defer wg.Done()

  for {

    time.Sleep(time.Second)
    fmt.Println("Inside myFunc1")
  }
}
```

189

```go
func myFunc2(wg *sync.WaitGroup) {

  defer wg.Done()

  for{

    time.Sleep(time.Second)
    fmt.Println("Inside myFunc2")
  }

}
```

Output(s):
Inside main
Inside myFunc1
Inside myFunc2
Inside myFunc1
Inside myFunc2
    ....

Example-11.8: In this example, we use the same function for three go-routines.

```go
package main                                          Code
import "fmt"                                          11.12
import "sync"
import "time"

var wg sync.WaitGroup

func main() {

  wg.Add(3) // 3 go-routines

  for i := 1; i <= 3; i++ {

    go myRoutine(i)
  }

  wg.Wait()

  fmt.Println("The main program finishes")
}
```

```
func myRoutine(i int) {

  defer wg.Done() // 3

  for cnt :=0; cnt < 3; cnt++ {

    time.Sleep(time.Second)
    fmt.Printf("Inside routine %v \n", i)
    fmt.Printf("Count for routine %v is %v \n", i, cnt)

  }

  fmt.Printf("The routine %v is finished\n", i)
}
```

Output(s):
Inside routine 2
Inside routine 1
Count for routine 1 is 0
Inside routine 3
Count for routine 3 is 0
Count for routine 2 is 0
Inside routine 2
Inside routine 1
Count for routine 1 is 1
Inside routine 3
Count for routine 3 is 1
Count for routine 2 is 1
Inside routine 2
Count for routine 2 is 2
The routine 2 is finished
Inside routine 1
Count for routine 1 is 2
The routine 1 is finished
Inside routine 3
Count for routine 3 is 2
The routine 3 is finished
The main program finishes

11.3 Go Channels

Go channels are objects and go-routines communicate with each other using channel objects.

When data is sent to a channel, the send statement is blocked until sent data is read by some go routines. In similar manner, when data is read from a channel, the read statement is blocked till any other go-routine writes data to the channel.

A bidirectional channel can be declared as

<pre><code>var channelName chan dataType</code></pre>

A bidirectional channel can also be declared using the make() function as

<pre><code>channelName := make(chan dataType)</code></pre>

The uni-directional channels can be declared using the make() function based on their directions as

send only channel
<pre><code>channelName := make(chan <- dataType)</code></pre>
receive only channel
<pre><code>channelName := make(<- chan dataType)</code></pre>

11.3.1 Buffered Channel in Go

Buffered channels have declared capacity values. When the buffered channel is used to send a value, the sending go-routine does not block if the channel is not full. In a similar manner, when a value sent from a buffered channel is received, the receiving go-routine does not block until the buffered channel is empty. A buffered bidirectional channel is declared as

<pre><code>channelName := make(chan dataType, capacity)</code></pre>

Buffered uni-directional channels are declared as

<pre><code>channelName := make(chan <- dataType, capacity)</code></pre>

<pre><code>channelName := make(<- chan dataType, capacity)</code></pre>

In the previous section, the make() function is used to declared un-buffered channels.

Un-buffered channels do not have capacities. When the un-buffered channel is used to send a value, the sending go-routine blocks until another go-routine receives the value. In a similar manner, when a value sent from an un-buffered channel is received, the receiving go-routine does block until another value is sent by the sender go-routine.

Example-11.9: In this example, we declare channels using **var** keyword.

```
package main                                          Code
import "fmt"                                           11.13

func main() {

  var cnlA chan int // bi-directional
  var cnlB chan <- int // send only
  var cnlC <- chan  int // receive only

  fmt.Printf("ChannelA value: %v \n", cnlA)
  fmt.Printf("ChannelA type: %T \n\n",cnlA)

  fmt.Printf("ChannelB value: %v \n", cnlB)
  fmt.Printf("ChannelB type: %T \n\n",cnlB)

  fmt.Printf("ChannelC value: %v \n", cnlC)
  fmt.Printf("ChannelC type: %T \n",cnlC)
}
```

Output(s):
ChannelA value: <nil>
ChannelA type: chan int

ChannelB value: <nil>
ChannelB type: chan<- int

ChannelC value: <nil>
ChannelC type: <-chan int

Example-11.10: In this example, we declare channels using **:=** operator.

```
package main                                          Code
import "fmt"                                           11.14

func main() {

  cnlA := make(chan int)
  cnlB := make(chan <- int)
  cnlC := make(<- chan  int)

  fmt.Printf("ChannelA value: %v \n", cnlA)
  fmt.Printf("ChannelA type: %T \n\n",cnlA)

  fmt.Printf("ChannelB value: %v \n", cnlB)
  fmt.Printf("ChannelB type: %T \n\n",cnlB)

  fmt.Printf("ChannelC value: %v \n", cnlC)
  fmt.Printf("ChannelC type: %T \n",cnlC)
}
```

Output(s):
ChannelA value: 0xc00007a060
ChannelA type: chan int

ChannelB value: 0xc00007a0c0
ChannelB type: chan<- int

ChannelC value: 0xc00007a120
ChannelC type: <-chan int

Send operation: The send operation is used to send data from one go-routine to another one, and the send operation is performed as

$$ch \text{ <- } val$$

where ch is the channel and val is the data value send to channel.

Receive operation: The receive operation is used to get the data sent, the receive operation is performed as

$$varName \text{ := } \text{<- } ch$$

where `varName` is the variable name and ch is the channel.

Example-11.11:

```
ch := make(chan int) //ch is an integer type channel       Code
ch <- val // send statement                                11.15
val = <- ch // receive statement

ch := make(chan string) // ch is a string type channel
ch <- "World" // sending value to the channel ch
```

Example-11.12: In this example, we create a buffered channel and send values through channel.

```
package main                                    Code
import "fmt"                                     11.16

func main() {

  ch := make(chan int, 2)

  ch <- 16
  ch <- 45

  fmt.Println("Received number:", <-ch)
  fmt.Println("Received number:", <-ch)
}
```

Output(s):
Received number: 16
Received number: 45

Example-11.13: We repeat the previous example for an un-buffered channel.

```
package main                                    Code
import "fmt"                                     11.17

func main() {

  ch := make(chan int)

  ch <- 16
  ch <- 45

  fmt.Println("Received number:", <-ch)
  fmt.Println("Received number:", <-ch)
}
```

Output(s):
fatal error: all goroutines are asleep - deadlock!

Example-11.14: In this example, we use go-routines which have channels in their arguments.

```
package main                                    Code
import "fmt"                                     11.18
import "time"

func main() {

  ch1 := make(chan string)

  go myRoutine1(ch1)
  go myRoutine2(ch1)

  time.Sleep(time.Second) // 1 sec delay

  close(ch1)

  fmt.Println("Terminating main")
}
func myRoutine1(ch chan string) {
  ch <- "Hello World1"
  ch <- "Hello World2"
}
func myRoutine2(ch chan string) {
  fmt.Println("Received message:", <- ch)
}
```

195

In Code-11.18, myRoutine1 has two send statements, however myRoutine2 has only one receive statement, for this reason, only "Hello World1" is displayed.

Output(s):
Received message: Hello World1
Terminating main

If the routines in Code-11.18 are written as in Code-11.19, then we get the outputs

Received message: Hello World1
Received message: Hello World2
Terminating main

```
func myRoutine1(ch chan string) {          Code
                                           11.19
  ch <- "Hello World1"
  ch <- "Hello World2"
}

func myRoutine2(ch chan string) {

  fmt.Println("Received message:", <- ch)
  fmt.Println("Received message:", <- ch)
}
```

Example-11.15: The Code-11.18 can be written as in Code-11.20 using sync.WaitGroup object.

```
package main                               Code
import "fmt"                               11.20
import "sync"

var wg sync.WaitGroup

func main() {

  wg.Add(2) // there are 2 go-routines

  ch1 := make(chan string)

  go myRoutine1(ch1)
  go myRoutine2(ch1)

  wg.Wait()

  close(ch1)

  fmt.Println("Terminating main")
}
```

```
func myRoutine1(ch chan string) {          Code
                                           11.20
  defer wg.Done()

  ch <- "Hello World1"
  ch <- "Hello World2"
}
func myRoutine2(ch chan string) {

  defer wg.Done()

  fmt.Println("Received message:", <- ch)
  fmt.Println("Received message:", <- ch)
}
```

Output(s):
Received message: Hello World1
Received message: Hello World2
Terminating main

Note that in Code-11.20, if close(ch1) is written before wg.Wait(), error arises. Since, channel is closed before the completion of go-routines.

Example-11.16: In this example, go-routine1 generates 3 random integers and sends them to the channel. The go-routine2 receives the integers from channel and prints them.

```
package main                               Code
import "fmt"; import "sync"                11.21
import "time"; import "math/rand"

var wg sync.WaitGroup

func main() {

  wg.Add(2) // there are 2 go-routines

  ch1 := make(chan int)

  go myRoutine1(ch1)
  go myRoutine2(ch1)

  wg.Wait()
  close(ch1)
  fmt.Println("Terminating main")
}
```

```go
func myRoutine1(ch chan int) {

  defer wg.Done()

  for indx :=0; indx < 3; indx++ {
    rand.Seed(time.Now().UnixNano())
    randInt := rand.Intn(200) // generate random integer in [0 200)

    ch <- randInt
  }
}
func myRoutine2(ch chan int) {

  defer wg.Done()

  for indx :=0; indx < 3; indx++ {
    fmt.Printf("Received integer: %d \n", <- ch)
  }
}
```

To generate the random integers we included "math/rand" package in our program, and we used rand.Intn(N) function to generate random integers in the interval $[0, N-1)$. We used the expression rand.Seed(time.Now().UnixNano()) to change the seed and generate different random numbers at each run of the program.

Output(s):
Received integer: 81
Received integer: 87
Received integer: 47
Terminating main

Example-11.17: In this example, we use unbuffered channel with anonymous go-routines.

```go
package main
import  "fmt"
import  "time"

func main() {

  ch1 := make(chan int)

  go func() {

    for indxN := 0; indxN < 5; indxN++ {
      ch1 <- indxN
    }
  }()
```

Code
11.22

```go
go func() {

  for indxM := 0; indxM < 5; indxM++ {

    fmt.Println("Received:", <- chl)
  }

}()

time.Sleep(time.Second)
}
```

Output(s):
Received: 0
Received: 1
Received: 2
Received: 3
Received: 4

Example-11.18: In this example, we use buffered channel with anonymous go-routines.

```go
package main                                Code
import "fmt"                                11.23
import "sync"

var wg sync.WaitGroup

func main() {

  wg.Add(2)

  chl := make(chan int, 5)

  go func() {

    for indxN := 0; indxN < 5; indxN++ {

      chl <- indxN
    }

    wg.Done()

  }()
```

```go
go func() {

   for indxM := 0; indxM < 5; indxM++ {

      fmt.Println("Received:", <- chl)
   }

      wg.Done()

   }()

   wg.Wait()
}
```

Output(s):
Received: 0
Received: 1
Received: 2
Received: 3
Received: 4

11.3.2 Using a Loop with a Channel

The range keyword can be used with channels. You get the values sent through the channel with the range keyword.

Example-11.19: In this example, we use range keyword for a buffered channel inside main function.

```go
package main                                    Code
import "fmt"                                     11.24

func main() {

   chl := make(chan int, 2)

   chl <- 56
   chl <- 67

   close(chl)

   for i := range chl {

      fmt.Println("Number:", i)
   }

}
```

Buffered channels can hold a number of values. When we use the keyword range for a buffered channel, the values will be received until the buffer is empty. Besides, channel should be closed.

If un-buffered channel is used in Code-11.24, i.e., if we use

$$chl := make(chan int)$$

then the program gives error " fatal error: all goroutines are asleep - deadlock!"

Example-11.20: In this example, we use range keyword in a for-loop to receive the sent values from a go-routine.

```
package main                                    Code
import "fmt"                                     11.25

func myRoutine(ch chan int) {

  ch <- 14
  ch <- 56
  ch <- 78
  ch <- 89

  close(ch)
}

func main() {

  chl := make(chan int)

  go myRoutine(chl)

  for num := range chl {

    fmt.Println("Received number:", num)
  }
}
```

The sender should close the channel as shown in yellow color in Code-11.25, otherwise, for-loop cannot now the number of elements sent.

Output(s):
Received number: 14
Received number: 56
Received number: 78
Received number: 89

Example-11.21: In this example, the go-routine has an infinite loop and it sends values through the channel. The values are received using a for-loop in the main part.

```
package main                                    Code
import "fmt"                                     11.26
import "time"

func myRoutine(ch chan int) {

   for {

      ch <- time.Now().Second()

      time.Sleep(time.Second)
   }
}

func main() {

   ch1 := make(chan int)

   go myRoutine(ch1)

   for sec := range ch1 {

      fmt.Println("Time in second:", sec)
   }
}
```

Output(s):
Time in second: 58
Time in second: 59
Time in second: 0
Time in second: 1
Time in second: 2
        ....

11.3.3 Range and Close

A channel can be tested by the receiver whether it has been closed or not by using a second parameter in receive expression as

$$value, \ status \ := \ <-ch$$

where status is false if the channel is closed and there are no more values to receive.

The loop

```
for val := range ch {

  // statements

}
```

receives values from the channel in a repeated manner until the channel is closed. Note that the channel can be closed by the sender only, never by the receiver. Panic arises if data sending is performed on a closed channel. Channels are different than files, files must be closed before the termination of the main program, however, channel can stay open, it is not a must to close the channels as files. Closing is only necessary to inform the receiver that there are no more values to be sent. For example, to terminate a range loop, channel closure information is used.

11.4 Select Statement in Go

Select statement is similar to the switch statement, and it is used for multiple channel operations. The select statement blocks, i.e., waits, until one of the cases is ready to communicate, i.e., to send or receive.

It chooses one of the cases at random if there are multiple cases ready. The syntax of the select statement is as

```
select {

    case send_or_receive_exp1:
      // statements1

    case send_or_receive_exp2:
      // statements2

    case send_or_receive_exp3:
      // statements3

    case send_or_receive_exp4:
      // statements4

    default default_statements:
    // default statements
}
```

Example-11.22: In this example, we will write a program to illustrate the use of the select statement. First let's write two go-routines as in Code-11.27. Inside each routine, a random delay is created.

```
package main                                                    Code
import "fmt"                                                    11.27
import "time"
import "math/rand"

func myRoutine1(ch1 chan string) {

  rand.Seed(time.Now().UnixNano())
  rn :=rand.Intn(1000) // generate random integer in [0 1000]
  time.Sleep(time.Duration(rn) * time.Millisecond) //random delay
}

func myRoutine2(ch2 chan string) {

  rand.Seed(time.Now().UnixNano())
  rn :=rand.Intn(1000)
  time.Sleep(time.Duration(rn) * time.Millisecond) //random delay
}
```

After the delay a message is sent through a channel by each go-routine as in Code-11.28. Each routine uses a different channel to send the message.

```
package main                                                    Code
import "fmt"                                                    11.28
import "time"
import "math/rand"

func myRoutine1(ch1 chan string) {

  rand.Seed(time.Now().UnixNano())
  rn :=rand.Intn(1000) // generate random integer in [0 1000]
  time.Sleep(time.Duration(rn) * time.Millisecond) //random delay

  ch1 <- "Channel-1"
}

func myRoutine2(ch2 chan string) {

  rand.Seed(time.Now().UnixNano())
  rn :=rand.Intn(1000)
  time.Sleep(time.Duration(rn) * time.Millisecond) //random delay

  ch2 <- "Channel-2"
}
```

In Code-11.29, we write the main part of the program. Channels and go-routines are declared inside main function.

```
package main                                                    Code
import "fmt"                                                    11.29
import "time"
import "math/rand"

func myRoutine1(ch1 chan string) {

  rand.Seed(time.Now().UnixNano())
  rn :=rand.Intn(1000) // generate random integer in [0 1000)
  time.Sleep(time.Duration(rn) * time.Millisecond) //random delay

  ch1 <- "Channel-1"
}

func myRoutine2(ch2 chan string) {

  rand.Seed(time.Now().UnixNano())
  rn :=rand.Intn(1000)
  time.Sleep(time.Duration(rn) * time.Millisecond) //random delay

  ch2 <- "Channel-2"
}

func main(){

  ch11:= make(chan string)
  ch12:= make(chan string)

  go myRoutine1(ch11)
  go myRoutine2(ch12)
}
```

Finally, select statement is added to the program as in Code-11.30.

```
package main                                                    Code
import "fmt"                                                    11.30
import "time"
import "math/rand"

func myRoutine1(ch1 chan string) {

  rand.Seed(time.Now().UnixNano())
  rn :=rand.Intn(1000) // generate random integer in [0 1000)
  time.Sleep(time.Duration(rn) * time.Millisecond) //random delay

  ch1 <- "Channel-1"
}
```

```go
func myRoutine2(ch2 chan string) {

  rand.Seed(time.Now().UnixNano())
  rn :=rand.Intn(1000)
  time.Sleep(time.Duration(rn) * time.Millisecond) //random delay

  ch2 <- "Channel-2"
}

func main(){

  ch11:= make(chan string)
  ch12:= make(chan string)

  go myRoutine1(ch11)
  go myRoutine2(ch12)

  select{

    case v1:= <- ch11:
      fmt.Println("Operating channel is:", v1)

    case v2:= <- ch12:
      fmt.Println("Operating channel is:", v2)
  }
}
```

When Code-11.30 is run depending on the random delays generated, different channels are used and different messages are displayed by the select statement.

The default case can be added to the select statement as in Code-11.31. Since go-routines need some time to execute, if we do not add another delay in main part as shown in yellow in Code-11.31, every time the program is run, the message at the default case will be printed. With the delay in the main part every time the program is run a random message will be seen at the output.

```go
package main                                          Code
import "fmt"                                          11.31
import "time"
import "math/rand"

func myRoutine1(ch1 chan string) {

  rand.Seed(time.Now().UnixNano())
  rn :=rand.Intn(1000) // generate random integer in [0 1000)
  time.Sleep(time.Duration(rn) * time.Millisecond) //random delay

  ch1 <- "Channel-1"
}
```

```go
func myRoutine2(ch2 chan string) {

  rand.Seed(time.Now().UnixNano())
  rn :=rand.Intn(1000)
  time.Sleep(time.Duration(rn) * time.Millisecond) //random delay

  ch2 <- "Channel-2"
}

func main(){

  ch11:= make(chan string)
  ch12:= make(chan string)

  go myRoutine1(ch11)
  go myRoutine2(ch12)

  rand.Seed(time.Now().UnixNano())
  rn :=rand.Intn(1000) // generate random integer in [0 1000)
  time.Sleep(time.Duration(rn) * time.Millisecond) //random delay

  select{

    case v1:= <- ch11:
      fmt.Println("Operating channel is:", v1)

    case v2:= <- ch12:
      fmt.Println("Operating channel is:", v2)

    default:
      fmt.Println("No channel operates")
  }

}
```

11.5 Mutex in Golang

In this section we explain mutex functions which are used to write race free go programs.

11.5.1 Race Condition for Go-Routines

Race condition may happen when shared resources are used by more than one go-routine. For instance assume two go-routines process one global variable, and one of the go-routine increments the value of global variable and the other go-routine decrements the global variable, so what will be the result?

In this case, a race condition arises; the winner will be the value which arrives to the digital gate outputs the first. Propagation delays of the gates cause the race problem. Mutex function of go language can be used to prevent the races.

Example-11.23: Let's illustrate the race condition by an example. First, let's declare a global variable initialized to zero, and a sync.WaitGroup variable as in Code-11.32.

```
package main                                    Code
import "fmt"                                     11.32
import "sync"

var glob_var int = 0
var wg sync.WaitGroup
```

Let's write two go-routines as in Code-11.33. One go-routine increments the global variable, and the other decrements the same global variable.

```
package main                                    Code
import "fmt"                                     11.33
import "sync"

var glob_var int = 0
var wg sync.WaitGroup

func routineInc() {

  for indx :=0; indx < 100000; indx++{

    glob_var++
  }

  wg.Done()
}
func routineDec() {

  for indx :=0; indx < 100000; indx++{

    glob_var--
  }

  wg.Done()
}
```

In Code-11.34, we write the main part of the program.

```
package main
import "fmt"
import "sync"

var glob_var int = 0
var wg sync.WaitGroup

func routineInc() {

  for indx :=0; indx < 100000; indx++{

    glob_var++
  }

  wg.Done()
}
func routineDec() {

  for indx :=0; indx < 100000; indx++{

    glob_var--
  }

  wg.Done()
}
func main() {

  wg.Add(2) // two go-routines

  go routineInc()
  go routineDec()

  wg.Wait()

  fmt.Println("Value of glob_var:", glob_var)
}
```

Code 11.34

When Code-11.34 is run many times, we see that at each different run we see a different output, for Example-11.23:

Value of glob_var: -21522
Value of glob_var: -6747
Value of glob_var: 31999

The different outputs are due to the race condition on shared global variable.

To prevent the race condition in Code-11.34, we can use the mutex function Lock() and Unlock(). For this purpose, we first declare a mutex variable as shown in yellow color in Code-

11.35 and then we can place mutex Lock() and Unlock() functions to the beginning and end of the go-routines as shown in yellow color in Code-11.35. The main part of the Code-11.35 stays the same.

```go
package main                                          Code
import "fmt"                                          11.35
import "sync"

var glob_var int = 0

var wg sync.WaitGroup

var m sync.Mutex

func routineInc() {

  // lock
    m.Lock()

    for indx :=0; indx < 100000; indx++{

      glob_var++
    }
    // unlock
    m.Unlock()

  wg.Done()
}
func routineDec() {
    // lock
    m.Lock()

    for indx :=0; indx < 100000; indx++{

      glob_var--
    }

    // unlock
    m.Unlock()

    wg.Done()
}
```

With the added changes in Code-11.35, when the program is run multiple times, we always get the output

Value of glob_var: 0

In Code-11.35, the mutex variable **m** is defined as the global variable. We can define the mutex variable inside main function as local variables. In this case, the implementations of the routines are done as in Code-11.36.

```go
package main                               Code
import "fmt"                               11.36
import "sync"

var glob_var int = 0

var wg sync.WaitGroup

func routineInc(m* sync.Mutex) {
 // lock
  m.Lock()

  for indx :=0; indx < 100000; indx++{

    glob_var++
  }
  // unlock
  m.Unlock()

  wg.Done()
}
func routineDec(m* sync.Mutex) {
  // lock
  m.Lock()

  for indx :=0; indx < 100000; indx++{

    glob_var--
  }

  // unlock
  m.Unlock()

  wg.Done()
}
func main() {

  var m sync.Mutex // local mutex variable
  wg.Add(2)

  go routineInc(&m)
  go routineDec(&m)

  wg.Wait()

  fmt.Println("Value of glob_var:", glob_var)
}
```

11.5.2 Atomic Operations in Golang

Atomic methods/functions perform race-free operations. Atomic methods/functions perform better and bring less overhead to the compiler when compared to the use of mutex functions. To be able to use the atomic method/function, we must include the package "sync/atomic" in our program.

One of the atomic functions which performs race free integer addition is the atomic.AddInt32() function with prototype

```
func AddInt32(addr* int32, delta int32) (new int32)
```

which performs race-free addition operation

$$*addr = *addr + delta$$

$$new = *addr$$

Example-11.24: The Code-11.34 suffers from race problem. In Code-11.37, we use atomic.AddInt64() atomic operation for increment and decrement operations, and race problem is eliminated.

```
package main                                    Code
import "fmt"                                     11.37
import "sync"
import "sync/atomic"

var glob_var1 int64 = 0
var glob_var2 int64 = 0
var wg sync.WaitGroup

func routineInc() {

  for indx :=0; indx < 100000; indx++{

    atomic.AddInt64(&glob_var1, 1) //glob_var++
    glob_var2++
  }
  wg.Done()
}
func routineDec() {

  for indx :=0; indx < 100000; indx++{

    atomic.AddInt64(&glob_var1, -1)  //glob_var--
    glob_var2--
  }
  wg.Done()
}
```

```go
func main() {

   wg.Add(2) // two go-routines
   go routineInc()
   go routineDec()
   wg.Wait()

   fmt.Println("Value of glob_var1:", glob_var1 )
   fmt.Println("Value of glob_var2:", glob_var2 )
}
```

When the Code-11.37 is run, we get the outputs

Value of glob_var1: 0
Value of glob_var2: -5841

The prototypes of a number of atomic methods/functions are given below

```go
func AddInt32(addr* int32, delta int32) (new int32)
func AddInt64(addr* int64, delta int64) (new int64)
func AddUint32(addr* uint32, delta uint32) (new uint32)
func AddUint64(addr* uint64, delta uint64) (new uint64)

func AddUintptr(addr* uintptr, delta uintptr) (new uintptr)

func CompareAndSwapInt32(addr* int32, old, new int32) (swapped bool)
func CompareAndSwapInt64(addr* int64, old, new int64) (swapped bool)
func CompareAndSwapPointer(addr* unsafe.Pointer, old, new
unsafe.Pointer) (swapped bool)
func CompareAndSwapUint32(addr* uint32, old, new uint32) (swapped
bool)
func CompareAndSwapUint64(addr* uint64, old, new uint64) (swapped
bool)
func CompareAndSwapUintptr(addr* uintptr, old, new uintptr) (swapped
bool)

func LoadInt32(addr* int32) (val int32)
func LoadInt64(addr* int64) (val int64)
func LoadPointer(addr* unsafe.Pointer) (val unsafe.Pointer)
func LoadUint32(addr* uint32) (val uint32)
func LoadUint64(addr* uint64) (val uint64)
func LoadUintptr(addr* uintptr) (val uintptr)

func StoreInt32(addr* int32, val int32)
func StoreInt64(addr* int64, val int64)
func StorePointer(addr* unsafe.Pointer, val unsafe.Pointer)
func StoreUint32(addr* uint32, val uint32)
func StoreUint64(addr* uint64, val uint64)
func StoreUintptr(addr* uintptr, val uintptr)
```

213

```go
func SwapInt32(addr* int32, new int32) (old int32)
func SwapInt64(addr* int64, new int64) (old int64)
func SwapPointer(addr* unsafe.Pointer, new unsafe.Pointer) (old
unsafe.Pointer)
func SwapUint32(addr* uint32, new uint32) (old uint32)
func SwapUint64(addr* uint64, new uint64) (old uint64)
func SwapUintptr(addr* uintptr, new uintptr) (old uintptr)
```

Methods

```go
type Bool
func (x* Bool) CompareAndSwap(old, new bool) (swapped bool)
func (x* Bool) Load() bool
func (x* Bool) Store(val bool)
func (x* Bool) Swap(new bool) (old bool)


type Int32
func (x* Int32) Add(delta int32) (new int32)
func (x* Int32) CompareAndSwap(old, new int32) (swapped bool)
func (x* Int32) Load() int32
func (x* Int32) Store(val int32)
func (x* Int32) Swap(new int32) (old int32)


type Int64
func (x* Int64) Add(delta int64) (new int64)
func (x* Int64) CompareAndSwap(old, new int64) (swapped bool)
func (x* Int64) Load() int64
func (x* Int64) Store(val int64)
func (x* Int64) Swap(new int64) (old int64)


type Pointer
func (x* Pointer[T]) CompareAndSwap(old, new *T) (swapped bool)
func (x* Pointer[T]) Load() *T
func (x* Pointer[T]) Store(val *T)
func (x* Pointer[T]) Swap(new *T) (old *T)


type Uint32
func (x* Uint32) Add(delta uint32) (new uint32)
func (x* Uint32) CompareAndSwap(old, new uint32) (swapped bool)
func (x* Uint32) Load() uint32
func (x* Uint32) Store(val uint32)
func (x* Uint32) Swap(new uint32) (old uint32)


type Uint64
func (x* Uint64) Add(delta uint64) (new uint64)
func (x* Uint64) CompareAndSwap(old, new uint64) (swapped bool)
func (x* Uint64) Load() uint64
func (x* Uint64) Store(val uint64)
func (x* Uint64) Swap(new uint64) (old uint64)


type Uintptr
func (x* Uintptr) Add(delta uintptr) (new uintptr)
```

```
func (x* Uintptr) CompareAndSwap(old, new uintptr) (swapped bool)
func (x* Uintptr) Load() uintptr
func (x* Uintptr) Store(val uintptr)
func (x* Uintptr) Swap(new uintptr) (old uintptr)

type Value
func (v* Value) CompareAndSwap(old, new any) (swapped bool)
func (v* Value) Load() (val any)
func (v* Value) Store(val any)
func (v* Value) Swap(new any) (old any)
```

Example-11.25: In this example, we illustrate the use of the atomic.LoadInt32() and atomic.LoadInt64() functions.

```
package main                          Code
import "fmt"                          11.38
import "sync/atomic"

func main() {

  var a int32 = 678
  var b int64 = 546

  at := atomic.LoadInt32(&a)
  bt := atomic.LoadInt64(&b)

  fmt.Println(at)
  fmt.Println(bt)
}
```

Example-11.26: In this example, we illustrate the use of the atomic.StoreInt32() function.

```
package main                          Code
import "fmt"                          11.39
import "sync/atomic"

func main() {

  var a int32

  atomic.StoreInt32(&a, 567)

  fmt.Println("a =", atomic.LoadInt32(&a))
}
```

Example-11.27: In this example, we use WaitGroup functions with atomic.AddInt32() function.

```
package main                                Code
import "fmt"                                11.40
import "sync"
import "sync/atomic"

func main() {

  var a int32
  var wg sync.WaitGroup

  for indx := 0; indx < 35; indx += 1 {

    wg.Add(1)

    go func() {
      atomic.AddInt32(&a, 1)
      wg.Done()
    }()

  }

  wg.Wait()
  fmt.Println("Atomic Variable Value:", a)
}
```

Output(s):
Atomic Variable Value: 35

Problems

1) Write two functions which display the message, "msg1", "msg2", and call them as go-routines in main() function. Run the program and see the output.

2) Fill in the dots in Code-11.41 with WaitGroup functions.

```
package main                                    Code
import "fmt"                                     11.41
import "sync"

var wg sync.WaitGroup

func main() {

    ...

    go myFunc()

    fmt.Println("Inside main function")

    ...
}

func myFunc() {

    ...

    fmt.Println("Inside myFunc")
}
```

3) Fill in the dots in Code-11.42.

```
package main                                Code
import "fmt"                                11.42
import "sync"

func main() {

    var wg sync...

    wg.Add...

    go myFunc(...)

    fmt.Println("Inside main function")

    wg.Wait...
}

func myFunc(...) {

    defer wg.Done()

    fmt.Println("Inside myFunc")
}
```

4) Define a string channel and send and receive the message "Hello" through this channel.

5) Fill in the dots in Code-11.43.

```
package main                                Code
import "fmt"                                11.43

func main() {

    chl := make(chan int, 3)

    chl <- 56
    chl <- 67
    chl <- 89

    close(chl)

    // print channel values using for-loop
    // with range keyword
}
```

6) Create a buffered channel and using this channel send and receive three string messages and print the received messages to the screen.

7) Find the mistakes in Code-11.44.

```go
package main                                    Code
import "fmt"                                    11.44

func myFunc(ch chan string) {

  ch <- "AA"
  ch <- "BB"
  ch <- "CC"
  ch <- "DD"
}

func main() {

  ch := make(chan string)

  go myFunc(ch)

  for val := range ch {

    fmt.Println(val)
  }
}
```

Chapter-12

File Operations in Go

Abstract: Files are used to store permanent data. In this chapter, we explain file operations used in Go language. Go has a rich set of file functions which are used to read and write files. Go file functions are available in the packages **os** and **io**. We need to include these packages in our programs to be able to use file processing functions. In Go, some of the file read and write functions automatically create and close the files eliminating the need of explicitly opening and closing the files, and this makes life easier for code developers.

12.1 File Functions

As in every programming language, files can also be processed in Go programming using some of the functions. The prototypes of the most commonly used functions for file processing are:

```go
func Create(fileName string) (*File, error)
func NewFile(fd uintptr, fileName  string) *File
func Open(fileName  string) (*File, error)
func OpenFile(fileName  string, flag int, perm FileMode) (*File,
error)
func (fp *File) Chdir() error
func (fp* File) Chmod(mode FileMode) error
func (fp* File) Chown(uid, gid int) error
func (fp* File) Close() error
func (fp* File) Read(b []byte) (n int, err error)
func (fp* File) ReadAt(b []byte, off int64) (n int, err error)
func (fp *File) Seek(offset int64, whence int) (ret int64, err error)
func (fp* File) Stat() (FileInfo, error)
func (fp* File) Write(b []byte) (n int, err error)
func (fp* File) WriteString(s string) (n int, err error)
```

12.2 Empty File Creation

We can use the function os.Create(), to create a new empty file in Go. The function os.Create() creates a new file if it does not exist, with the file mode 0666, for reading and writing. If the file exists the contents of the file are erased without deleting the file, which is called truncation. The returned file descriptor is used for reading and writing. If there is a problem in file creation, then the function returns an error of type *os.PathError.

220

Example-12.1: In Code-12.1, a text file with name "myFile.txt" is created using os.Create() function.

```
package main                                          Code
import "fmt"                                          12.1
import "log"
import "os"

var fp* os.File
var myError   error

func main() {

  fp, myError = os.Create("myFile.txt")

  if myError != nil {

    log.Fatal(myError)

  } else {

    fmt.Printf("File %s is created successfully: ",  fp.Name())

  }
}
```

Output(s): File myFile.txt is created successfully:

Example-12.2: The program in Code-12.1 can be written as in Code-12.2 without declaring the variables using the keyword var.

```
package main                                          Code
import "fmt"                                          12.2
import "log"
import "os"

func main() {

  fp, myError := os.Create("myFile.txt")

  if myError != nil {

    log.Fatal(myError)

  } else {

    fmt.Printf("File %s created successfully: ",  fp.Name())

  }

  fp.Close()// close the file

}
```

12.3 Check if a File Exists in Go

To check whether a file exists in Go or not we use the function os.Stat() function for the file. If the function returns the os.ErrNotExist error, then the file does not exist otherwise it exists.

Example-12.3: In Code-12., we use os.Stat() function to check the existence of a file.

```
package main                                    Code
import "fmt"                                     12.3
import "os"

func main() {

  _, myErr := os.Stat("myFile.txt")

  if os.IsNotExist(myErr) {

    fmt.Println("File does not exist")

  } else {

    fmt.Println("File exists")

  }
}
```

12.4 Deleting a File in Go

To delete a file in Go, we use the function os.Remove(). If the to be deleted does not exist, the function os.Remove() returns an error of type *os.PathError.

Example-12.4: In Code-14., we use os.Remove() function to delete a file.

```
package main                          Code
import "fmt"                           12.4
import "os"
import "log"

func main() {

  myErr := os.Remove("myFile.txt")

  if myErr != nil {

    log.Fatal(myErr)
  }

  fmt.Println("File is deleted")
}
```

12.5 Getting File Info

We use os.Stat() function to read the file information. Go directories are also files and os.IsDir() function is used to check if a file is used as a directory or as a storage file.

Example-12.5: In Code-12., we use os.Stat() function to get information about a file.

```
package main                                          Code
import "fmt"                                           12.5
import "os"
import "log"

func main() {

  fp, myErr := os.Stat("myFile.txt")

  if myErr != nil {
    log.Fatal(myErr)
  }

  fmt.Println("File name: ", fp.Name())
  fmt.Println("File size in bytes: ", fp.Size())
  fmt.Println("File permissions: ", fp.Mode())
  fmt.Println("File is last modified: ", fp.ModTime())
  fmt.Println("Is directory: ", fp.IsDir())
}
```

Output(s):

File name: myFile.txt

File size in bytes: 0

File permissions: -rwxrwxrwx

File is last modified: 2023-09-18 17:34:35.21185683 +0000 UTC

Is directory: false

The file returned can be either a self-contained file or a it can be a directory containing other files. In Code-12.5, the function fp.IsDir() returns false if the file is not a directory containing other files.

12.6 Opening Files

In Section 12.2, we explained Create() function which is used to create a non-existing files. Files can be opened using a variety of functions. In this section, we explain some of the functions used for file opening. These functions can be used to open an already existing file, or they can be used to create a non-existing file as well.

12.6.1 Open() Function

The prototype of the Open() function is as

```
func Open(name string) (*File, error)
```

This function is used to open a file for reading only. Once the file is opened it can be used for reading; and the associated file descriptor has mode O_RDONLY.

If there is an error in opening the file, error message is generated.

Example-12.6: In Code-12.6., we use os.Open() function to open a file for reading only.

```
package main                                    Code
import "fmt"                                     12.6
import "log"
import "os"

func main() {

  fp, myError := os.Open("myFile.txt")

  if myError != nil {

    log.Fatal(myError)

  } else {

    fmt.Printf("File %s is opened successfully",  fp.Name())
  }

  fp.Close()// close the file

}
```

12.6.2 OpenFile()Function

The prototype of the OpenFile() function is as

```
func OpenFile(name string, flag int, perm FileMode) (*File, error)
```

The function OpenFile() is used to open a file with specified flag, e.g., O_RDONLY etc.

If the file does not exist, and the O_CREATE flag is passed, it is created with the indicated FileMode. The most commonly used FileMode codes are as

```
os.FileMode = 0777  // FullAccess, AllPermission
os.FileMode = 0755  // OwnerCanDoAllExecuteGroupOtherCanReadExecute
os.FileMode = 0644  // OwnerCanReadWriteGroupOtherCanReadOnly
os.FileMode = 0744  // OwnerCanDoAllGroupOtherCanReadOnly
os.FileMode = 0766  // OwnerCanDoAllGroupOtherCanReadWriteOnly
os.FileMode = 0711  // OwnerCanDoAllGroupOtherCanExecuteOnly
os.FileMode = 0755  // OwnerCanDoAllGroupOtherCanReadExecuteOnly
os.FileMode = 0722  // OwnerCanDoAllGroupOtherCanWriteOnly
```

Flag parameter can contain one of

```
os.O_RDONLY  // open the file read-only.
os.O_WRONLY  // open the file write-only.
os.O_RDWR    // open the file read-write
```

which can be ORed with

```
os.O_APPEND // append data to the file when writing.
os.O_CREATE  // create a new file if none exists.
os.O_EXCL    // used with O_CREATE, file must not exist.
os.O_SYNC    // open for synchronous I/O.
os.O_TRUNC   // truncate regular writable file when opened.
```

to control the behavior.

Example-12.7: In Code-17., we use os.OpenFile() function to open a file.

```
package main                                              Code
import "fmt"                                               12.7
import "log"
import "os"

func main() {

  fp, myErr := os.OpenFile("myFile.txt", os.O_RDWR |os.O_CREATE, 0755)

  if myErr != nil {

    log.Fatal(myErr)

  } else {

    fmt.Printf("File %s is opened successfully",  fp.Name())
  }

  fp.Close()
}
```

12.7 Writing to File

File writing can be achieved in different ways using one of the io, os, and ioutil packages. The package ioutil is deprecated in Go1.16.

12.7.1 Conventional Approach Using the os Package

In conventional approach

- we first create a file for writing
- then, we write the file and close the file,
- since closing an open file before terminating the program is a critical issue, we can use defer function to close the file immediately after we open it.

Example-12.8: In this example, we use os package functions Write(), WriteString() and WriteAt() for file writing.

```go
package main
import "fmt"
import "os"

func main() {

  fp, myErr := os.Create("myFile.txt")

  if myErr != nil {
    fmt.Println(myErr)
  }
  // order file close
  defer fp.Close()

  fp.Write( [] byte ("AAAA") ) // write the file

  // write a string
  fp.WriteString("\nBBBB")

  // write from a specific offset
  fp.WriteAt( [] byte ("CCCC"), 15)  // 15 is the offset from start
}
```

Code 12.8

When Code-12.8 is run, we get the file myFile.txt

```
                    myFile.txt

AAAA

BBBB......CCCC
```

Example-12.9: In this example, we create the file using OpenFile() and use the function Write() for file writing.

```
package main                                              Code
import "os"                                               12.9
import "log"

func main() {

  fp, myErr := os.OpenFile("myFile.txt", os.O_WRONLY, 0644)

  if myErr != nil {

    log.Fatal(myErr)
  }

  defer  fp.Close()

  fp.Write([] byte("Hello World!"))
}
```

12.7.2 File Writing Using the ioutil Package

The arguments of ioutil.WriteFile() function contains the file path, the data to write, and the file mode. If the file doesn't exist, it is created. If the file already exists, it is overwritten.

Example-12.10: In this example, we use ioutil package functions WriteFile() for file writing.

```
package main                                            Code
import "fmt"                                             12.10
import "log"
import "io/ioutil"

func main() {

  d := [] byte("Hello World!")

  myErr := ioutil.WriteFile("myFile.txt", d, 0644)

  if myErr != nil {

    log.Fatal(myErr)

  } else {

    fmt.Println("Data is successfully written to file")

  }
}
```

12.7.3 File Writing Using the io Package

Example-12.11: In this example, we use WriteString() function of io package for file writing.

```go
package main                                    Code
import "io"                                      12.11
import "os"
import "log"

func main() {

  fp, myErr := os.Create("myFile.txt")

  if myErr != nil {
    log.Fatal(myErr)
  }

  defer fp.Close()

  io.WriteString(fp, "Hello World!")
}
```

12.7.4 Buffered File Writing

If small amount of data is written to a file repeatedly, it can negatively affect the performance of the program, since, each write creates an overhead to the system, and if immediate file update is not required, it is a good idea to stock small amount of data and write it to the file when the stock size goes beyond a definite size (the default size is 4096 bytes) or the Flush() method is called.

So it is critical to call Flush() function when sufficient amount of data is collected in the buffer to start writing.

Example-12.12: Let's illustrate the buffered file writing with an example. First, let's create a file and orders its close in advance using defer() function as in Code-12.12.

```go
package main                                    Code
import "bufio"                                   12.12
import "os"
import "log"

func main() {

  // Open file for writing

  fp, myErr := os.Create("myFile.txt")
```

228

```
    if myErr != nil {

        log.Fatal(myErr)

    }
    defer fp.Close()
}
```

We create a buffer from file pointer, fp, using bufio.NewWriter () function and write the data to the buffer using Write() function as in Code-12.13.

```
myBuffer := bufio.NewWriter(fp)                                    Code
                                                                   12.13
writtenSize, myErr := myBuffer.Write( [] byte{45, 34, 43, 76} )

if myErr != nil {

  log.Fatal(myErr)
}
log.Printf("Written size (bytes): %v \n", writtenSize)
```

We can write a string using WriteString() function to the buffer as in Code-12.14.

```
writtenSize, myErr = myBuffer.WriteString("Hello World \n")   Code
                                                             12.14
if myErr != nil {
  log.Fatal(myErr)
}
log.Printf("Written size (bytes): %v \n", writtenSize)
```

We are using default buffer size which is 4096 bytes. The used buffer size and empty buffer size can be determined using Available() function, and we can write the data in the buffer to the file using the Flush() function as in Code-12.15.

```
bufferSize := myBuffer.Buffered()                          Code
                                                           12.15
log.Printf("Bytes buffered: %d\n", bufferSize)

freeSize := myBuffer.Available()

if myErr != nil {
  log.Fatal(myErr)
}

log.Printf("Available buffer: %d\n", freeSize)

myBuffer.Flush()
}
```

If we concatenate all the codes up to this point and run the entire program we get the file myFile.txt and at the screen we have the outputs

2023/09/22 20:40:00 Written size (bytes): 4
2023/09/22 20:40:00 Written size (bytes): 13
2023/09/22 20:40:00 Bytes buffered: 17
2023/09/22 20:40:00 Available buffer: 4079

If new data is to be written to the file using buffer, we can reset the buffer first and repeat the same steps as in Code-12.16.

```
myBuffer.Reset(myBuffer)                                  Code
                                                          12.16
freeSize = myBuffer.Available()

if myErr != nil {
  log.Fatal(myErr)
}

log.Printf("Free buffer buffer: %d\n", freeSize)

// write data to the buffer here

myBuffer.Flush()  // write the buffered data to the file
```

After buffer reset, we can change the size of the buffer using NewWriterSize() function as in Code-12.17.

```
myBuffer = bufio.NewWriterSize( myBuffer, 12000 )         Code
                                                          12.17
  freeSize = myBuffer.Available()

  if myErr != nil {
    log.Fatal(myErr)
  }

  log.Printf("Available buffer: %d\n", freeSize)
}
```

12.7.4 Writing Binary Data to a File

Binary data to the files can be written using Write() function of the binary package.

230

Example-12.13: In this example, we illustrate how to write a struct object into a binary file. First let's declare a struct as in Code-12.18.

```
package main
import "encoding/binary"
import "fmt"
import "os"
import "log"

type myStr struct {

        a int32
        b float32

}
```
Code 12.18

Next, we create a file as in Code-12.19.

```
package main
import "encoding/binary"
import "fmt"
import "os"
import "log"

type myStr struct {

        a int32
        b float32
}

func main() {

  fp, myErr := os.Create("data.bin")

  if myErr != nil {

        log.Fatal(myErr)
  }

  defer fp.Close()
}
```
Code 12.19

The struct object can be written to the binary file as in Code-12.20.

```go
func main() {                                          Code
                                                       12.20
  fp, myErr := os.Create("data.bin")

  if myErr != nil {

      log.Fatal(myErr)
  }
  defer fp.Close()

  var s = myStr{45, 67}
  myErr = binary.Write(fp, binary.LittleEndian, s)

  if myErr != nil {

      log.Fatal(myErr)

  } else {

      fmt.Println("Object is written to the file successfully")
  }
}
```

12.8 File Reading

File reading in Go can be performed in a number of different ways. In this section, we explain file reading methods in go programming.

12.8.1 Reading All the File Using the ioutil Package

This method is not an efficient to read large files. It is preferred for small files. The function ReadFile() of the package ioutil is used to read the file. The file is automatically opened and it is closed automatically after reading. So, explicit opening, closing are not needed.

Example-12.13: In this example, we use ReadFile() function of the ioutil package to read a file.

```go
package main                               Code
import "fmt"                               12.21
import "io/ioutil"
import "log"

func main() {

  dat, myErr := ioutil.ReadFile("myFile.txt")

  if myErr != nil {

      log.Fatal(myErr)
  }
```

```
    fmt.Printf("Data read: %v \n",dat)
    fmt.Printf("Data read: %s \n",dat)
}
```

```
                        myFile.txt
    Hello World


```

Output(s):

2023/09/23 11:04:25 Data read: [72 101 108 108 111 32 87 111 114 108 100]
2023/09/23 11:04:25 Data read: Hello World

Data read: [72 101 108 108 111 32 87 111 114 108 100]
Data read: Hello World

12.8.2 Read File by Chunks

In this method, exactly n bytes are read from the file at each call of the ReadFull() function.

Example-12.14: In this example, we use ReadFull() function of the io package to read a file.

```
package main                                        Code
import "fmt"                                         12.22
import "io"
import "log"
import "os"

func main() {

  fp, myErr := os.Open("myFile.txt")

  if myErr != nil {
      log.Fatal(myErr)
  }

  chunk := make([]byte, 4)
  readSize, myErr := io.ReadFull(fp, chunk)

  fmt.Printf("Number of bytes read: %d\n", readSize)
  fmt.Printf("Data read: %s \n\n", chunk)
```

```
readSize, myErr = io.ReadFull(fp, chunk)

fmt.Printf("Number of bytes read: %d\n", readSize)
fmt.Printf("Data read: %s\n", chunk)
}
```

12.8.3 Reading Binary File

Functions used for binary files are available in the package "encoding/binary". The Read() function of the binary package is used to read binary data from a binary file.

Example-12.15: The binary file created in Code-12.20 can be read by the program in Code-12.23.

```
package main                                            Code
import "encoding/binary"                                12.23
import "fmt"
import "os"
import "log"

type myStr struct {

        a int32
        b float32
}

func main() {

  fp, myErr := os.Open("data.bin")

  if myErr != nil {

        log.Fatal(myErr)
  }

  st := myStr{}

  binary.Read(fp, binary.LittleEndian, &st.a)
  binary.Read(fp, binary.LittleEndian, &st.b)

  fmt.Println("a =", st.a)
  fmt.Println("b =", st.b)

  fp.Close()
}
```

Bibliography

1) https://go.dev/doc/

2) https://pkg.go.dev/

2) https://golangdocs.com/

Index

About the Author

Orhan Gazi is a professor of electrical and electronics engineering. He has been in academic world for more than 25 years. He is the author of 17 academic text books in different areas. Among the book he authored 10 of them were published by international publication houses. He is the author of Modern C Programming book.

Golang Programming

Learn Future Programming